Christmas is Coming! 1990

Compiled and Edited by Linda Baltzell Wright

Oxmoor House®

Contents

© 1990 by Oxmoor House, Inc.
Book Division of
Southern Progress Corporation
P.O. Box 2463
Birmingham, Alabama 35201

Library of Congress Catalog Card Number: 84-63030
ISBN: 0-8487-1016-9
ISSN: 0883-9077
Manufactured in the United States of America
First Printing

Executive Editor: Nancy J. Fitzpatrick
Production Manager: Jerry Higdon
Associate Production Manager: Rick Litton
Art Director: Bob Nance
Copy Chief: Mary Jean Haddin

Christmas Is Coming! 1990

Editor: Linda Baltzell Wright
Illustrator and Designer: Barbara Ball
Editorial Assistant: Alice L. Cox
Production Assistant: Theresa L. Beste
Copy Assistant: Susan Smith Cheatham
Photographers: John O'Hagan, Colleen Duffley,
  Mary-Gray Hunter, Melissa Springer
Photo Stylist: Connie Formby

To find out how you can order *Cooking Light*
magazine, write to *Cooking Light*®, P.O. Box
C-549, Birmingham, AL 35283

Children's Workshop: Happy Holiday Crafts

Trimmings to Fix

Presents to Make

Parents' Workshop: Great Gifts for Children

Grin and Wear It

Just for Fun

Designers & Contributors

A Word to Parents

Christmas and kids go together like peanut butter and jelly. That's why we've filled our pages with this magic combination. *CHRISTMAS IS COMING! 1990* is chockful of fun projects for kids. This year we've included *The Littlest Star,* an original play for your kids to do with friends or classmates. And whether it's performed in the garage or the auditorium, we think it will be a holiday treat for all involved.

Talented designers from all over the country again share their decoration and gift ideas in "Children's Workshop." Fun to make and easy to do, these projects will be hard to resist. You'll want to pull out your scissors and work right along with the kids as they make a flock of Button-Face Angels or a Christmas Brigade of cardboard soldiers. The gift ideas are simple, too. Children will love making a place mat for the family pet! And for grandparents, what could be better than a sponge-painted family tree?

And when the kids are tucked away for the night, turn to "Parents' Workshop" for gift ideas that will bring big smiles to little faces on Christmas morning. There are huggable toys and pull toys, a sweater to knit and shirts to stencil. There's even a dragon sleeping bag. So whether you like to use a needle and thread or hammer and nails, there's something for you—and for yours.

Dear Kids

Have you and your friends ever wanted to put on your own Christmas play? Turn to the first chapter in *Christmas Is Coming! 1990* to find a play written just for you. You can even make a program and tickets. And maybe you can talk somebody's Mom into helping you with costumes. Be sure to invite your friends and neighbors because your production is bound to be the hit of the holiday season.

When you're ready to deck the halls, you'll find lots of ideas in "Trimmings to Fix." Make a delicious garland for your tree. Just slip candy and straws onto a string. Paint your hands green and make a wreath for the mantel. Or try making your own Christmas cards this year. In

Tear It Up, you'll find three colorful cards you can make by just tearing and gluing paper. They're that easy to make.

Christmas wouldn't be Christmas without presents, and handmade presents are the best kind. So look through the pages in "Presents to Make," and you'll find everything from Funky Frames to Safety Pin Bracelets. There's sure to be something for just about everyone on your list.

But before you begin any of the projects, check with a grown-up to be sure it's a suitable one for you to make. The projects labeled Level 1 are the easiest. Level 2 projects are simple, too, but take longer to complete. The most difficult projects are labeled Level 3.

The Best Gift of All

At Christmas, we want to find the best gift of all for each special person. The play, *The Littlest Star,* is about just that—a very special gift for a very special baby. Call up friends on the block or at school and get together to do your own version of *The Littlest Star.* With the help of somebody's mom, you can make costumes and scenery. Photocopy the ticket and use it as an invitation. Copy the program and fill in the place, time, and names of the cast. Pass out the programs as your audience arrives. Then tell your guests to sit back and enjoy your gift to them this Christmas—it may be the best gift of all!

THE LITTLEST STAR

CAST

Narrator
Star
Angel
Malcolm, a shepherd boy
Zachary, another shepherd boy
Hannah, a shepherd girl
Three Wise Men
Joseph
Mary
Baby Jesus

NARRATOR: Step outside this Christmas Eve. If you look up into the winter sky and listen closely, you just might hear a case of first-night jitters. [Pauses for a second to listen to soft giggles behind the curtain.] It's not widely known, but on the first Christmas almost two thousand years ago, the littlest star had a very important job.

[Curtain opens. Small child dressed in white tights sits on a tiny ladder. Beside the ladder stands another child, a bit older, costumed as an angel. She is holding her favorite teddy bear.]

STAR: How do I look?

ANGEL: Very special, baby Star! I've *never* seen you look so sparkling.

STAR: [She beams.] Thanks. But I'm so nervous. What if I can't do it right? What if nobody even *sees* me?

ANGEL: Oh, little Star, you'll be brilliant! [Pause.] And besides, there's no need to worry. I'll be here to help you.

[Angel helps Star down the ladder. They exit to stage right, hand in hand, as two Shepherds enter with their sheep and blankets from stage left. The Shepherds stretch and yawn, then curl up to sleep with sheep and blankets.]

NARRATOR: "And there were in the same country shepherds abiding in the field, keeping watch over their flock by night. And, lo, the angel of the Lord came upon them, and the glory of the Lord shone round about them: and they were sore afraid. And the angel said unto them, Fear not: for, behold, I bring you good tidings of great joy, which shall be to all people. For unto you is born this day in the city of David a Saviour, which is Christ the Lord."

Luke 2: 8-11

[Hannah comes running in from stage left.]

HANNAH: Malcolm, Zachary, how can you sleep on such an important night? [They sit up, rubbing the sleep from their eyes, a little confused.] Didn't you hear the angel? A baby has been born in Bethlehem, and He is to be our King! Wake up! Wake up! Let's go find Him.

[Shepherds and Shepherdess exit stage left as Angel and Star enter from stage right and walk to center stage. Three Wise Men enter slowly from stage right. They appear to be grumbling and confused. They wander in the shadows while Angel and Star talk about them.]

STAR: [Confused] They're *still* lost! Why can't they see me?

[Wise Men continue to point in different directions in a confused state.]

ANGEL: Maybe they're just too tired. They *have* been traveling for days. On *camels*. Can you imagine?

STAR: I guess I'll just have to try to shine even brighter.

[Pointing in the direction of Bethlehem, she wrinkles her brow with total concentration. She exits stage left as Angel leads the way. The Wise Men continue to look lost until the Star is completely off-stage and a bright light flashes.]

WISE MEN: [Excitedly] There it is! This way!

[They exit toward the light, stage left. Curtain.]

[As Narrator reads, manger is put in place behind curtain. Joseph, Mary, and the Baby gather at the manger.]

14

NARRATOR: "And, lo, the star, which they saw in the east, went before them, till it came and stood over where the young child was. When they saw the star, they rejoiced with exceeding great joy. And when they were come into the house, they saw the young child with Mary his mother, and fell down, and worshipped Him: and when they had opened their treasures, they presented unto Him gifts."

Matthew 2: 9-11

[Curtain opens; Wise Men and Shepherds enter.]

JOSEPH: Thank you all for coming.

[Shepherds and Wise Men, one by one, present their own personal gifts to the Baby.]

ANGEL: [The Angel is the last one. After a goodbye kiss, she gives the Baby her teddy bear.] Happy birthday, Baby!

MARY: You're all so kind to bring such wonderful gifts.

[Star enters from stage left and edges toward the manger slowly, shuffling her feet, looking down.]

MARY: What's the matter, little Star?

STAR: I was so nervous getting all polished up, I forgot to bring a present for the Baby.

MARY: [Smiling.] Little Star, you brought the *best* present of all. Tonight the love from your heart made a path of light to guide others here. You were the brightest star of all.

[Star smiles proudly as cast sings a Christmas carol.]

THE END

Costume Creations

Use the pattern and instructions to make the basic robe for each character in the play except the star. Then check the list at the end for putting together each costume.

You will need (for each robe):
1¼ yards (45″-wide) brightly colored fabric for robe
Thread to match
½ yard (36″-wide) coordinating fabric for headdress

Note: Old bedspreads, sheets, dish towels, and fabric scraps make great costume materials. Bandannas, ropes, and old jewelry can be used as belts and headbands.

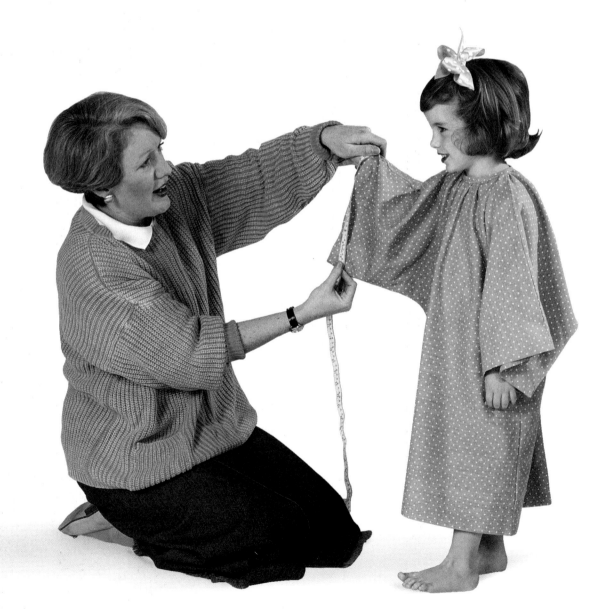

Making the Robes

1. Enlarge the pattern for the robe to the desired size (pattern includes ½″ seam allowances). Transfer all markings. Place the pattern on the fold and cut out 2, 1 for the robe front and 1 for the back.

2. With right sides facing and raw edges aligned, stitch the robe front to back along shoulder seams. Stitch the underarm and side seams. Clip curves. Turn right side out and press.

3. Cut a 5″ slit along the center fold on the front of the robe. Turn under the raw edges of the slit and around the neck opening. Machine-stitch a narrow hem.

4. Hem the sleeves and the robe to the desired length by machine.

Putting It All Together

Star
White turtleneck shirt, white tights, white sweatshirt, cardboard star, cardboard star wand, white ballet slippers

Angel
Pink robe, white eyelet collar, yellow halo, yellow cardboard wings

Shepherds and shepherdess
Robes, turtleneck shirts, dish towel headdresses, twisted fabric for headbands, flip-flop sandals, and sheep. (See Just for Fun for instructions for A Loveable Lamb.)

Wise Men
Corduroy robes, turtleneck shirts, scarves, high-top tennis shoes, roller skates, work boots, cardboard crowns, stocking caps, twisted fabric for headbands

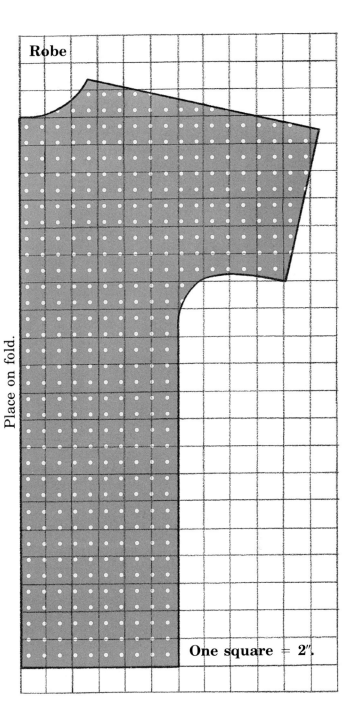

Robe

Place on fold.

One square = 2″.

Mary
Blue robe, turtleneck shirt, headdress, garland for her head, tennis shoes

Joseph
Robe, turtleneck shirt, striped headdress, twisted fabric for headband, staff, tennis shoes

Admit One

For special invitations for *The Littlest Star,* make copies of ticket and fill in all the important information. Then give the tickets to your guests. Tell them to present their tickets at the door.

Presents
"The Littlest Star.."
A play about the FIRST Christmas

TIME:_____

PLACE:_____

ADMIT ☆ one

Playbill

The program for *The Littlest Star* is called a *playbill.* It will be fun to make copies of it to hand out to your guests as they arrive. To save lots of time tracing, have an adult photocopy the program and cover for you. Fill in the names of the cast (who is in the play) and production staff (who helped with the play). Then everyone will know who's who. You can color the star on the cover, or stick a large star sticker on it. Fold the cover and the program on the broken lines. Then insert the program inside the cover.

☆ Act ONE
Angel and Star talk about
the Upcoming Event.

☆ Act Two
Shepherds and Wise Men are
guided by the Angel and Star.

☆ Act ThREE
The presentation of gifts
to the Baby Jesus.

All Sing.
_____   _____   _____

Thank you for coming.
May your Christmas
be a joyful one!

PLAYBILL

The
Littlest
Star

The Littlest Star

A play about the FIRST Christmas

CAST:

Narrator . . . .

Star . . . . . .

Angel . . . . . .

2 Shepherds

Shepherdess .

3 Wise Men .

Joseph . . . .

Mary . . . . .

Baby Jesus

Dog . . . .

Production Staff . . . .

Children's Workshop

Happy Holiday Crafts

Deer, Deer!

Red-nosed reindeer always rate at Christmas! So find your scissors, paper, and glue and make a pair or two.

You will need (for 1 reindeer):
Pencil
Tracing paper
Scissors
4″ x 8″ piece of brown paper
4″ x 4″ piece of green paper
1½″ x 1½″ piece of red paper
2″ x 1½″ piece of white paper
Scrap of black paper
Hole punch
Glue
⅓ yard red polka-dot ribbon

1. Trace and cut out the patterns.

2. Trace the head pattern 1 time and the ear pattern 2 times on brown paper. Cut them out. Trace the antler pattern 2 times on green paper. Cut them out. Cut 1 nose out of red paper. Cut out 2 circles from white paper for the eyes.

3. Use the hole punch to make 2 black circles for the pupils in the eyes.

4. Using the photograph as a guide, glue the ears and antlers to the back of the

26   *Level 1*

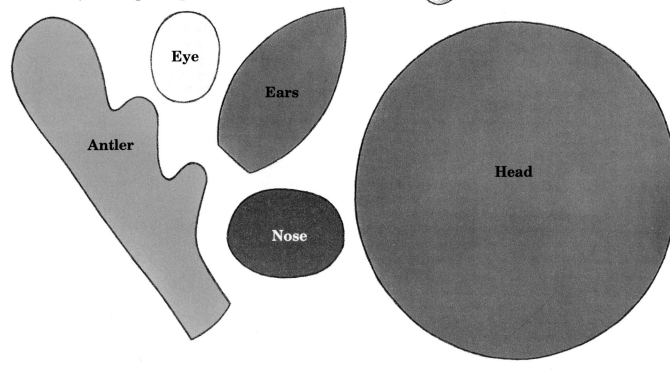

reindeer's head. Glue the white part of the eyes and then the black to the front of the head. Then glue on the nose.

5. To make a hanger, glue the ends of the ribbon to the back of the reindeer's head, creating a loop above the head.

Antler

Eye

Ears

Nose

Head

Christmas Brigade

Make these Christmas soldiers to parade around your tree this year.

You will need:
Newspaper
Paper towels
Pencil
Ruler
Scissors
Liquid starch
Large plastic bowl
Toilet paper rolls
Ornament hook
Blue, red, yellow, flesh, and white acrylic paint
Small paintbrushes
Black marker

1. Cover your work space with newspaper. Cover a separate drying area with newspaper.

2. Cut paper towels into 1½″-wide strips.

3. Mix equal amounts of water and liquid starch in the bowl. Dip each paper towel strip into the starch mixture.

4. Wrap the sides of the toilet paper roll with the strips, overlapping the ends of the strips. Cover the roll completely.

5. Make an X covering the top of the roll, with 2 of the paper towel strips.

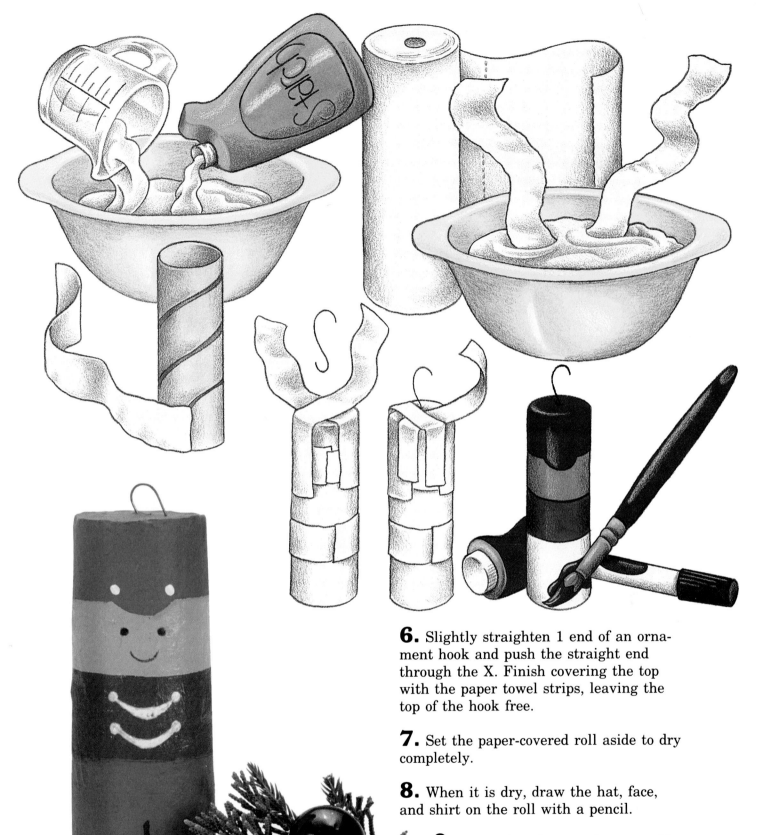

6. Slightly straighten 1 end of an ornament hook and push the straight end through the X. Finish covering the top with the paper towel strips, leaving the top of the hook free.

7. Set the paper-covered roll aside to dry completely.

8. When it is dry, draw the hat, face, and shirt on the roll with a pencil.

9. Using the photograph as a guide, paint the soldier. Let dry. Then make eyes, mouth, pants and feet with the marker.

Button-Face Angels

With their heavenly smiles, these angels are cute as a button!

You will need (for 3 angels):
Pencil
Scissors
Pink, yellow, and green felt scraps
Scraps of medium-weight interfacing
Pinking shears
Small scraps of fabric
Polyester stuffing
Straight pins
Tapestry needle
1½ yards brightly colored yarn
Red permanent marker
3 (1″) white 2-hole buttons
Glue
3 (6″) pieces of ribbon

1. Trace and cut out the patterns.

2. Cut the arms and legs from the pink felt. Cut the halo from the yellow felt. Cut the wings from interfacing.

3. For the body, choose the color you want. Use pinking shears to cut 2 felt or fabric triangles with notched edges.

4. Place a small piece of stuffing on 1 body triangle. Lay the matching triangle on top.

5. Pin the arms and legs so that they are held in place between the 2 body triangles.

6. Thread the tapestry needle with yarn. Sew around the body, being sure to catch the arms and legs in the stitches.

7. Use the red marker to draw a smile on the button. The 2 holes in the button are the angel's eyes. Glue the button head to the halo. Then set it aside.

8. For the hanger, fold the ribbon in half and glue the cut ends to the back of the body, near the top. Then glue the

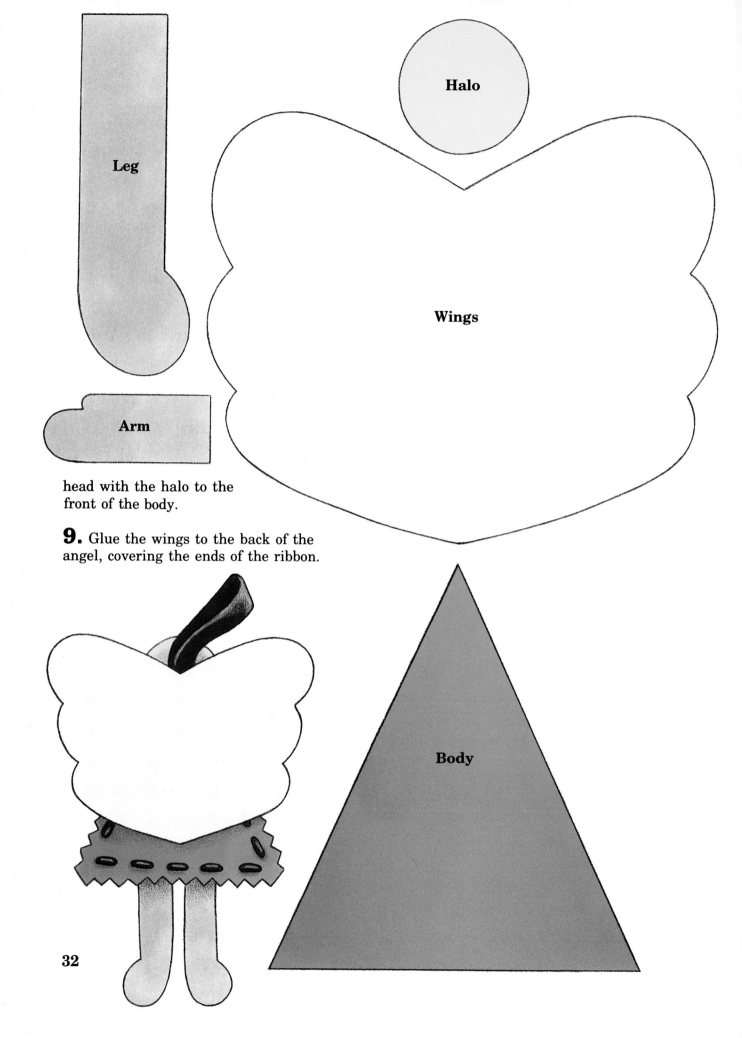

Leg

Halo

Wings

Arm

head with the halo to the
front of the body.

9. Glue the wings to the back of the
angel, covering the ends of the ribbon.

Body

Stars 'n Straws

You will need:
Pencil
Scissors
Yellow corrugated paper
2 different-colored plastic drinking straws
Hole punch
Colored string

1. Trace the star in the photograph. Cut out the pattern. Cut out the pattern. Trace the pattern on the yellow corrugated paper. Cut out the star.

2. Cut a small piece from each straw.

3. With the hole punch, punch a hole in the top of the star.

4. Run the string through the hole in the star. Adjust the string so that the ends are the same length. With the pieces of string together, slide the 2 straw pieces down over the string.

5. Make a big knot in the ends of the string so that the straws will not slide off.

String a simple star to hang upon your tree. It's so easy and quick to do, you'll want at least two or three.

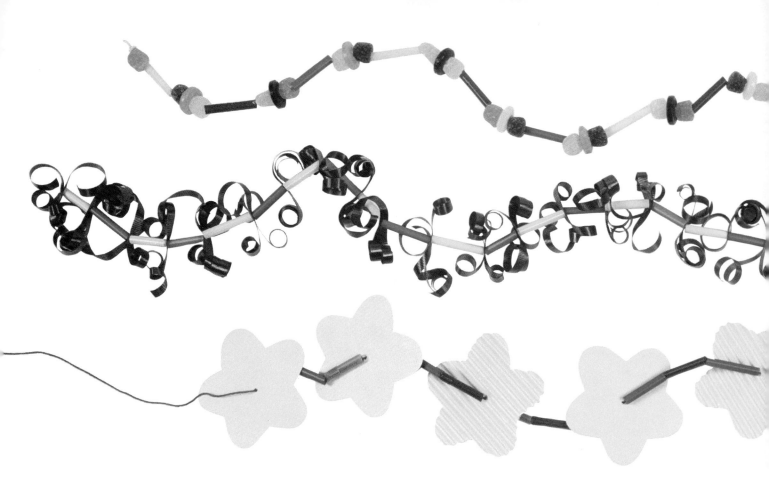

Straw Garlands

Sweeten your tree with a candy garland or add some sparkle with a string of stars.

Before you start: If you want to make longer garlands, just tie the 4-foot garland lengths together.

Star Garland

You will need:
Pencil
Tracing paper
Scissors
Yellow corrugated paper
Yellow poster board
Colored plastic drinking straws
Tapestry needle
String

1. Trace the star in the photograph on page 33. Cut out the pattern. Trace the pattern on poster board and on corrugated paper. Cut out the stars.

2. Cut the drinking straws into 2″ lengths.

3. Thread the needle with a 4-foot piece of string. Tie a big knot at the end. With the needle, poke a hole in the center of a star and run the needle and string through it. Then run the needle and string through 3 pieces of straw. Now run the needle and string through another star and 3 more straw pieces. Keep doing this until you are 6″ from the end of the string. Slide the needle off and tie a big knot in the end of the string.

Gumdrop Garland

You will need:
Colored plastic drinking straws
Scissors
Gumdrops
Fruit-flavored ring candies
Tapestry needle
String

1. Cut the drinking straws into 2″ lengths.

2. Thread the tapestry needle with a 4-foot piece of string. Tie a big knot at the end. Run the threaded needle through a gumdrop, ring candy, gumdrop, and piece of straw. Keep doing this until you are 6″ from the end of the string. Slide the needle off and tie a big knot in the end of the string.

Ribbon Garland

You will need:
Colored plastic drinking straws
Scissors
Red curling ribbon
Tapestry needle
String

1. Cut the drinking straws into 2″ lengths.

2. Cut the curling ribbon into 7″ pieces. Using the blades of the scissors, curl the ribbon pieces.

3. Thread the needle with a 4-foot piece of string. Tie a big knot at the end. Run the threaded needle through the center of 2 pieces of ribbon and through 1 piece of straw. Keep doing this until you are 6″ from the end of the string. Slide the needle off and tie a big knot in the end of the string.

36

Feathered Friends

Make two or three or even a flock of these birds. Hang some on your Christmas tree or let them nest in your holiday wreath.

You will need:
Pencil
Tracing paper
Scissors
Plastic plates with ribbed edges
Glue
Sequins
Hole punch
Ribbon

Level 1

1. Trace and cut out the patterns for the bird. Place the patterns on the plate, with the edges of the tail and wings on the ribbed edge of the plate. Place the bird pattern in the center of the plate. Cut out the pieces.

2. Cut the slits along the lines marked on each piece.

3. Slip the slits in the wings and the tail into the slits on the bird's body.

4. Glue sequin eyes on both sides of the bird's head.

5. Punch a hole at the X in the bird's back with the hole punch.

6. For a hanger, cut a piece of ribbon and pull it through the hole. Tie a knot in the ends.

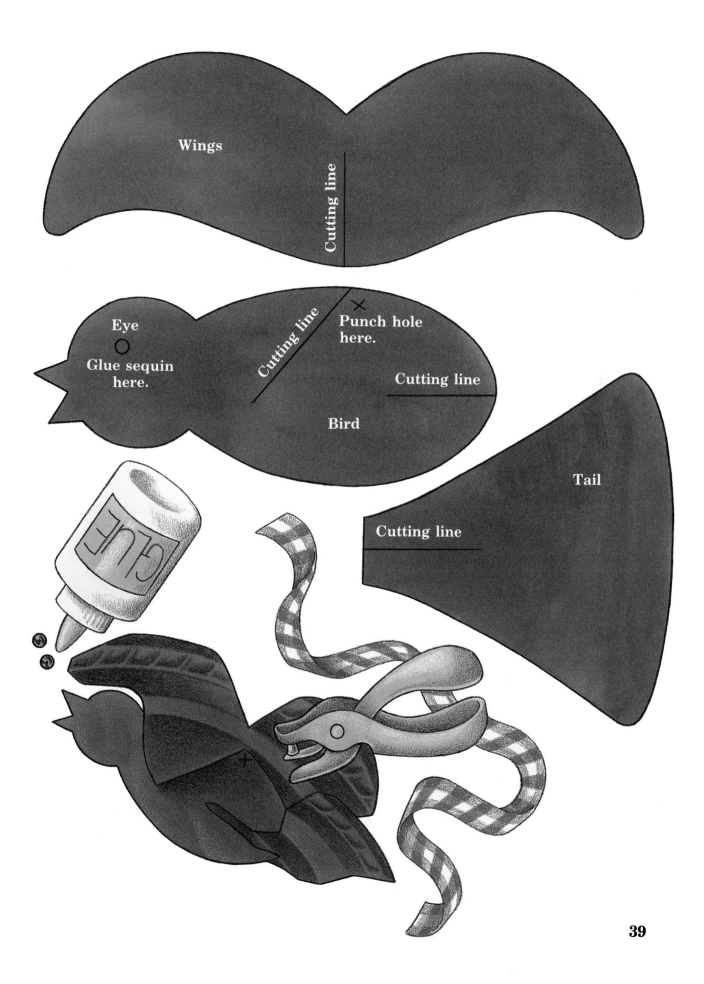

39

A Hands-Some Wreath

Here's a fun hands-on project for the family. You and the other kids can do the painting, and Mom or Dad can do the sewing.

You will need:
1 yard of cream-
  colored canvas
Pushpin and 13″ string
Pencil
Scissors
Green acrylic paint
Paintbrush
Green bias tape
Needle and thread
Polyester fiberfill
Roman shade ring for hanger
Paint pen

1. Make a compass with the string, pushpin, and pencil. Draw 2 circles on the canvas. Cut the string to 6″ and make a small circle in the center of each large circle.

2. Paint the palm of 1 of your hands. Then have your brothers and sisters each paint 1 of their palms. Taking turns, make handprints all around the front of the wreath.

3. Let the paint dry completely. Then cut out the wreath front and back.

4. Ask a grown-up to complete the wreath this way: Place the wrong sides of the wreath circles together with the raw edges aligned. Pin and baste the inner edges of the wreath circles together. Machine-stitch both edges of the bias tape over these raw edges.

5. Pin and baste the outer edges of the wreath circles together, leaving a 6″ opening. Stuff with polyester fiberfill; baste the opening closed. Machine-stitch both edges of bias tape over outer raw edges.

6. Have everyone who made a handprint use the paint pen to sign his or her name on the back of the wreath. Don't forget to add the date.

7. Sew the ring to the top back of the wreath for hanging.

Snowbuddies

Make boy and girl snowbuddies and add a smiling touch to a Christmas wrap.

You will need (to make both):
Pencil
Tracing paper
White poster board
Scraps of glossy wrapping paper: green, blue, yellow, red, black
Scissors
White glue
Heart stickers
Hole punch
Black felt-tipped marker
Yellow curling ribbon
6″ of blue satin ribbon

1. Trace and cut out all patterns.

2. Cut 2 bodies and 2 heads from white poster board. Cut 2 sweaters from green paper. Cut 4 mittens from blue paper. Cut 1 apron and 2 large buttons from yellow paper. Cut 2 narrow strips from red paper for suspenders. Cut 1 hat from red paper and 1 from black.

3. Glue 1 sweater to each body. Trim the suspenders to fit the boy. Then glue the suspenders and buttons on the boy's sweater. Glue the apron on the girl's sweater. Stick 3 heart stickers down the front of the apron. Glue mittens on both.

4. Punch 4 holes from blue paper and glue them in place for eyes. With the marker, draw eyelashes for the girl.

5. Cut 4 red circles for the cheeks. Glue in place. Add the smiles with the marker.

6. To make hair for the girl, cut 2 strands of curling ribbon, each 12″ long. Curl the ribbons with the scissors blade. Then glue them to the top of her head. Cut a slit in her hat where the line is on the pattern. Slip the hat over her head and glue in place. Tie the blue ribbon in a bow and glue on the hat. Glue the boy's hat on his head. Let the glue dry. Then glue the heads to the bodies. Let them dry.

7. Glue snowbuddies to packages.

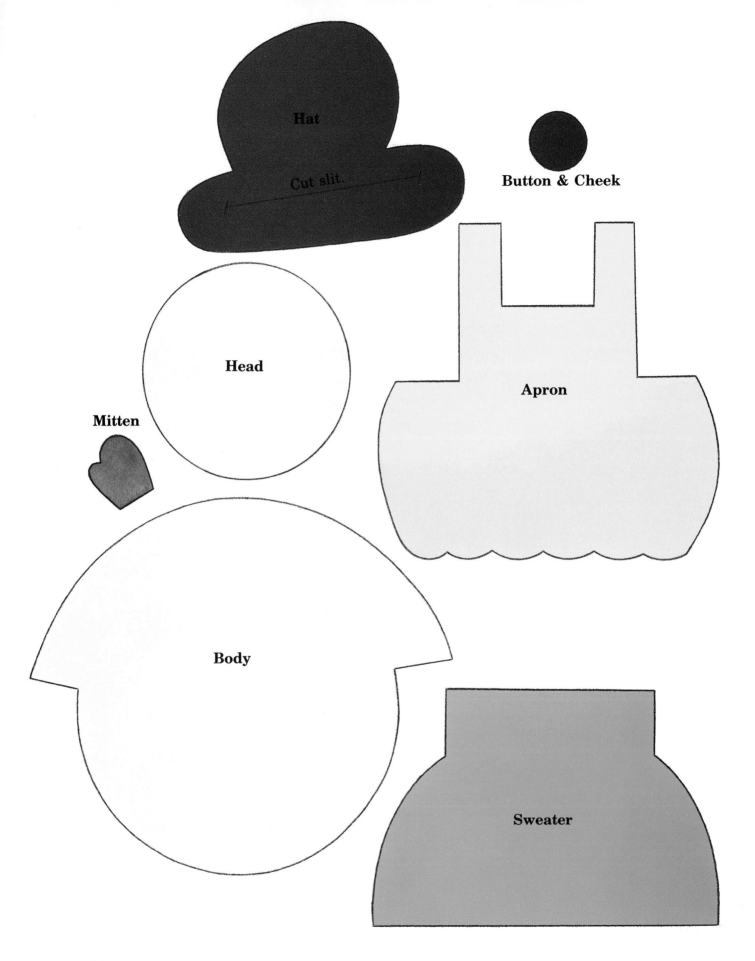

Hat

Cut slit.

Button & Cheek

Head

Apron

Mitten

Body

Sweater

44

Woven Santa Basket

Fill this Santa Basket with candy and trinkets and hang it on the tree. Or make lots of baskets as favors for everyone coming to Christmas dinner.

Level 3

You will need:
Tracing paper and pencil
White, pink, red, and green paper
Scissors
Glue
Black fine-tip marker

1. Trace and cut out the patterns. From white paper, cut 2 beards, 1 mustache, 2 eyebrows, and 1 tassel. From pink paper, cut 1 face. From red paper, cut 1 cap, 1 nose, and 1 mouth.

2. With 1 beard piece still folded, cut along the lines inside the pattern piece, but only as far as the pattern shows. Cut the other beard piece in the same way.

   With a pencil, lightly label the loops on both beards 1, 2, 3, 4, as shown. Label 1 beard piece A and the other B.

3. To make the basket with the beard pieces, we need to weave the beard pieces through and around one another, not just over and under each other. Lay the folded beard pieces with the rounded sides at right angles to each other. Slide the tip of loop 1A through loop 1B. Then slip 1A around loop 2B, through loop 3B, and around 4B. Push the completed row toward the rounded top of piece B. Now begin weaving with loop 2A. Slip 2A around loop 1B, then through 2B, and around 3B, and through 4B. Weave loop 3A in the same way as 1A and loop 4A in the same way as 2A. As you finish weaving push each loop against the loop above.

4. To finish the beard, cut 18 strips of white paper, ¾″ wide by 3″ long. Roll the strips tightly around a pencil to curl them. Glue 1 end of each curl to the outside edge of the back of the woven beard basket. Overlap the strips so that the beard is really filled out and curls around Santa's face. Let the glue dry.

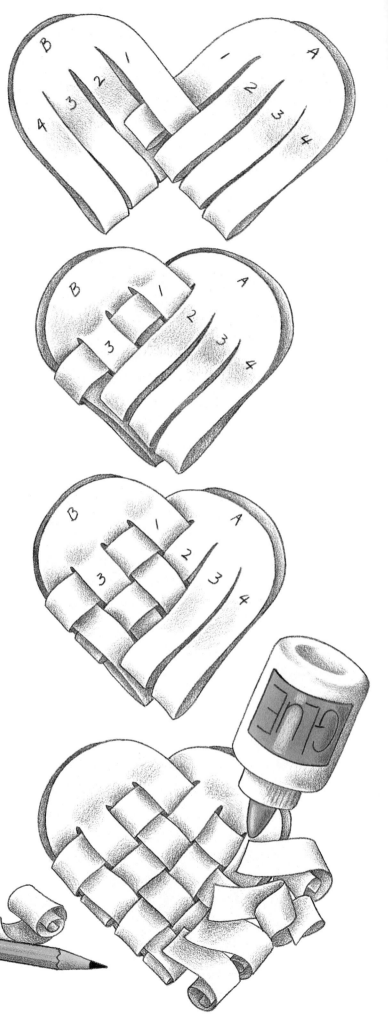

5. Glue the nose to the center top of the beard basket, letting it stick up a little above the beard. Center the mustache on bottom of the nose. Before gluing it, slip the mouth underneath the mustache at the center bottom. Glue both the mouth and mustache to the beard. Let dry.

6. Center the face on the cap and glue it in place. Let the glue dry. Open the beard basket. Glue the face and cap to the inside of the beard front, following the placement line on the pattern.

7. Draw the eyes and eyelashes with the marker, using the pattern as a guide. Glue the eyebrows where Santa's face meets his cap. Cut along the lines of the tassel for a spiral effect and glue it to the top of the cap.

8. For the hanger, cut a 1″ by 8″ strip from green paper. Glue 1 end to the back of the cap. Glue the other end inside the opposite side of the beard basket.

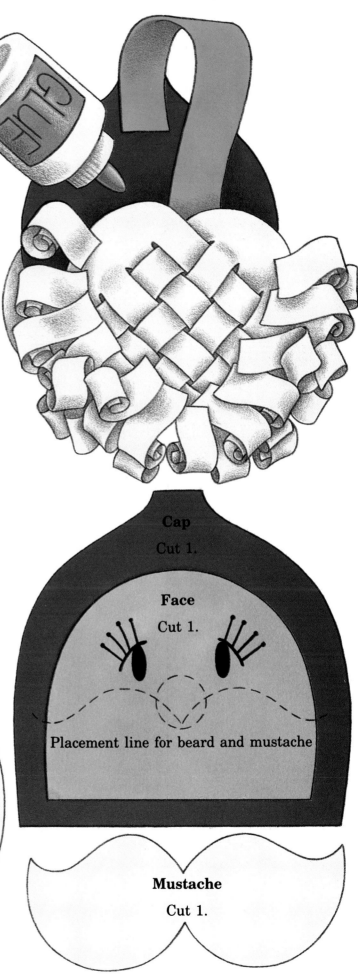

Nose
Cut 1.

Mouth
Cut 1.

Eyebrow
Cut 2.

Tassel
Cut 1.

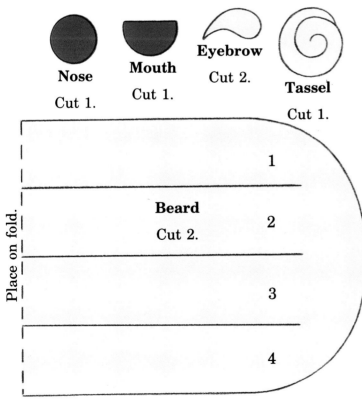

Place on fold.

Beard
Cut 2.

1

2

3

4

Cap
Cut 1.

Face
Cut 1.

Placement line for beard and mustache

Mustache
Cut 1.

Three Kings Card

On that first Christmas, the Three Kings wandered across desert sands following a new star. Let your kings travel across sandpaper to give a special texture to your handmade Christmas card.

You will need:
Pencil
White drawing paper
Scissors
Felt-tipped markers
Fine-tipped black marker
Brown construction paper
8½″ x 11″ piece of blue paper
Scrap of yellow paper
Glue
1 piece of fine and 1 piece of coarse
 sandpaper
3″ piece of fine twine

1. With 1 king going left and the other 2 going right, trace the king pattern 3 times onto drawing paper.

2. Color the kings, using felt-tipped markers. With the black marker, outline each king and add the details. Cut out the 3 kings.

3. Trace and cut out the camel pattern. With 1 camel facing left and the other 2 camels facing right, trace 3 camels onto brown construction paper. With the black marker, outline the camels and make eyes. Cut out the camels.

4. Fold the 8½″ x 11″ blue construction paper in half to measure 8½″ x 5½″. Trace the star pattern onto yellow paper and cut it out. Glue the star in the upper right corner.

5. Tear 2 hills from the fine sandpaper and 1 from the coarse sandpaper. Glue 1 fine sandpaper hill at the top of the card. Overlap and glue the coarse hill in the middle. Overlap and glue the other fine hill at the bottom. Trim the edges of the hills even with the card.

6. Cut 3 (1″) pieces of twine for tails. Glue a tail to the back of each camel.

7. Glue the kings and camels to the card as shown in the photograph.

8. With the black marker, draw a lead line from each king's hand to his camel. Then draw a halter on each camel.

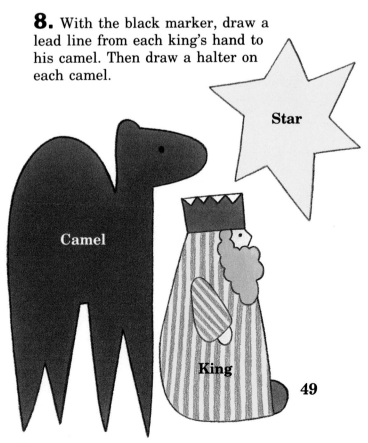

Star

Camel

King

49

Tear It Up

Tear, rip, and glue. These cards are so simple to do! Make one, make two—oh, go ahead and make a few.

You will need for 3 cards:
Construction paper for cards
Scraps of paper: pink, red, white, black, blue, yellow, green
Hole punch
White glue
Small red heart stickers
Gummed stars
Black felt-tip marker
Star garland
Strand of red paper excelsior

For Santa

1. Tear Santa's face from pink paper and his beard and hat trim from white. Tear his hat from red paper. Hole-punch eyes from black.

2. Glue 2 eyes on Santa's face. Glue Santa's face to his beard. Stick on a heart sticker for his nose.

3. Glue on the hat. Then glue the hat trim where Santa's face and hat meet.

4. Fold down the hat and stick a star onto the point.

5. Fold a piece of construction paper in half to make a card and glue Santa on the front.

For Angel

1. Tear the angel's face and legs from pink paper and her wings from white. Tear her dress and arms from blue. Tear yellow paper into strips for hair. Hole-punch eyes from green paper.

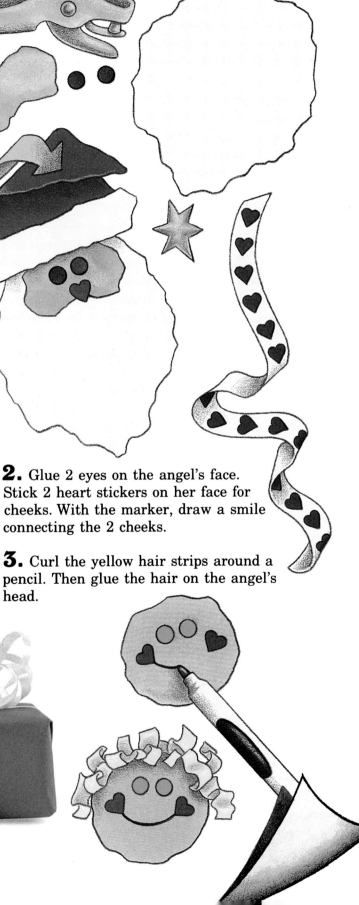

2. Glue 2 eyes on the angel's face. Stick 2 heart stickers on her face for cheeks. With the marker, draw a smile connecting the 2 cheeks.

3. Curl the yellow hair strips around a pencil. Then glue the hair on the angel's head.

For Tree

1. From green paper, tear a tree shape. From the other colored paper, tear small balls for ornaments and box shapes.

2. Fold a piece of construction paper in half to make a card and glue the tree on the front. Then glue on the colored ornaments. Use the red paper excelsior to make a garland and glue it in place.

3. Glue paper strips on the presents to look like ribbons. Then glue the presents under the tree.

4. Stick a star on the top of the tree.

4. Glue the angel's face to the wings. Lay the arms on the wings with hands in the air. (Glue just the top of the arms to the wings.) Then glue the dress over the arms and under the chin. Glue legs underneath the bottom of her dress.

5. Fold the arms down to the center and stick on a star.

6. Fold a piece of construction paper in half to make a card and glue the angel on the front. Cut a piece of star garland and bend it to make a halo with a stem. Tear the stars off the stem. Slip the stem between the card and the wings.

52

Winter Flurry Windsock

With their top hats and scarves, these snowmen are all ready for cold winter winds. But inside, their smiles will last till spring.

You will need:
10″ x 20″ piece of green pindot wrapping paper
10″ x 20″ piece of heavy paper
Glue
3 sheets of white construction paper
Scraps of red, black, pink, and orange construction paper
Scissors
Black fine-tip marker
Small circle, square, and heart stickers
Large star stickers
Yellow crepe paper
Clear tape
Hole punch
1 yard of ribbon

Level 3

Tearing, Cutting, and Gluing

1. Glue the green pindot paper to the heavy paper. Spread the paper on the table with the green side up.

2. Tear the white paper into 2 large balls for each snowman. Use 1 for the head and the other for the body. Make 3 snowmen. Space the snowmen evenly on the green paper and glue them in place.

3. Tear the red paper into 3 scarves. Glue 1 around each snowman's neck. Cut a big black rectangle for each top hat. Cut thinner rectangles for the brims. Glue a hat and brim on each snowman's head. Cut out pink circles for cheeks and glue them in place.

4. With the black marker, draw eyebrows, eyes or eyelashes, and dots for mouths on the snowmen.

5. For carrot noses, cut tiny triangles from orange paper. Glue them in place. Cut black strips for arms and glue them in place.

6. For buttons, stick 3 small stickers down the front of each snowman.

7. Tear small snowballs from the white paper and glue them around the bottom of the snowmen.

8. Add the star stickers wherever you want a shiny twinkle.

Assembling the Windsock

1. Turn the paper over so that the snowmen are face down. Cut the crepe paper into 20″ strips. Glue strips side by side across the bottom edge of windsock.

54

2. When all the glue is dry, roll the green paper into a tube with the snowmen on the outside. Tape the ends of the paper together on the inside and outside.

3. To make a hanger, punch 4 holes in the tube, ½″ from the top edge and 5″ apart. Cut the ribbon in half. String each piece through 2 holes and tie all 4 ends together at the top in a knot.

55

Santa Card Box

When the mailman arrives with Christmas cards, this Santa's arms will be ready and waiting.

You will need:
6″ x 9″ x 4″ cardboard box
Brown paper
Tracing paper
Pencil
Scissors

11″ x 14″ piece of white poster board
Scraps of red, red polka dot, and pale pink paper
Glue
Twine
Black marker

1. Cover the inside and outside of the box with brown paper.

2. Trace and cut out the patterns.

3. Draw around the large triangle pattern for Santa on the white poster board. Cut it out. Also cut out a circle from the poster board for the pom-pom on Santa's hat.

4. Cut the strip for the face from pink paper. Cut the hat and 2 mittens from polka dot paper. Cut the nose from red paper.

5. Glue the hat to Santa's head, matching the top points. Then glue the pom-pom to the point.

6. Measure 1¾″ below the hat on the poster board and glue on the face. (The white space is the trim on the hat.) Then glue the nose on the face. Use the black marker to make eyes.

7. Line up the bottom of Santa with the bottom of the box. Glue Santa to the back of the box. Then glue the mittens to the front of the box.

Level 2

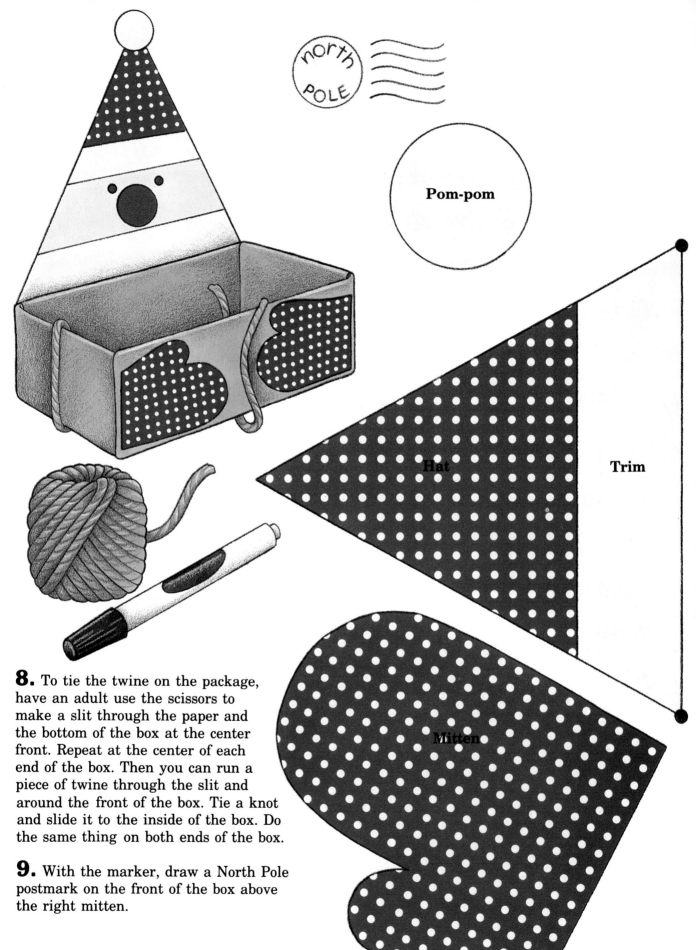

Pom-pom

Hat

Trim

Mitten

8. To tie the twine on the package, have an adult use the scissors to make a slit through the paper and the bottom of the box at the center front. Repeat at the center of each end of the box. Then you can run a piece of twine through the slit and around the front of the box. Tie a knot and slide it to the inside of the box. Do the same thing on both ends of the box.

9. With the marker, draw a North Pole postmark on the front of the box above the right mitten.

58

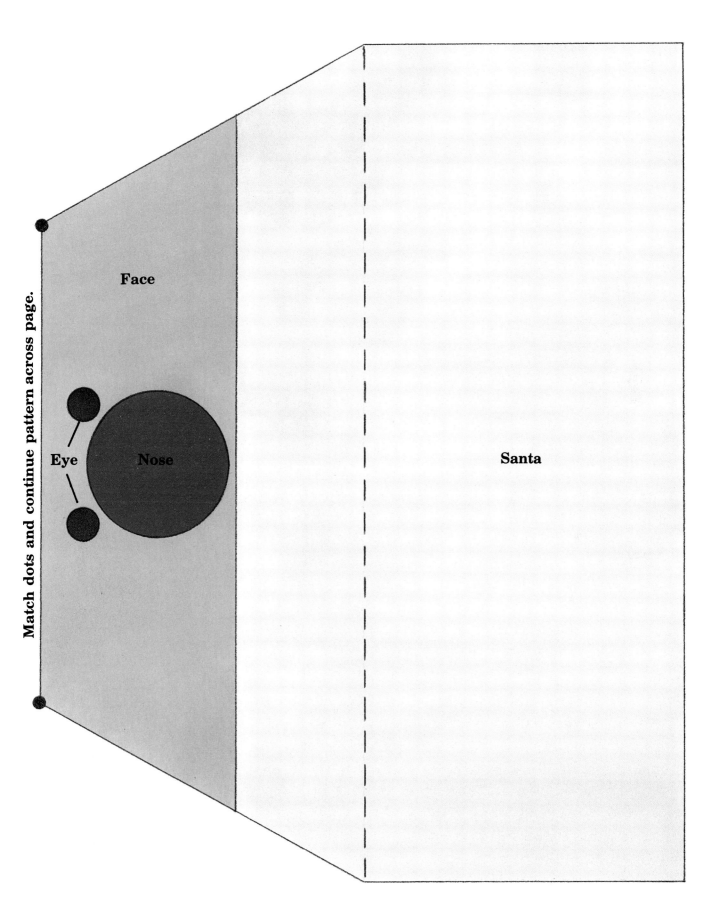

Match dots and continue pattern across page.

Face

Eye

Nose

Santa

Christmas Tree
Watering Can

Even a Christmas tree gets thirsty
and needs a drink of water. With this
watering can, somebody's tree will be
drinking in style.

You will need:
Watering can
Red acrylic spray paint
Newspaper
Pencil
Tracing paper
Scissors
Green acrylic paint
Paintbrush
Hole punch
Scraps of colored paper
Glue stick
Silver stars
Clear acrylic spray
24″ (1″-wide) ribbon

1. In a well-ventilated room, cover the floor with newspapers. Spray the watering can with red paint. Let dry.

2. Trace and cut out the tree pattern 3 times.

3. Line up the trees on 1 side of the watering can so that you can figure out how many trees will fit between the handle and the spout. Tape the trees in place and trace around them. Remove the patterns.

4. Paint the trees with the paintbrush and the green paint. To cover the red paint on the can, you will probably need at least 3 coats. Let the paint dry between coats.

5. Using the hole punch and colored paper, punch out about 10 colored balls for each tree. Glue the balls on the tree. Glue a silver star on the top of each tree.

6. Spray the watering can with the acrylic spray. Let dry.

7. Wrap the ribbon around the handle and tie it in a bow.

61

Pig E. Bank

Christmas is coming, the geese are getting fat, so you better put a penny in Pig E.'s back.

You will need:
Tracing paper
Pencil
Scissors
2 pieces of 8½″ x 11″ bright pink construction paper
8½″ x 11″ piece of black construction paper
Cardboard wrapping paper tube
Cardboard paper towel tube
Glue
Hole punch
Poster board
Black marker
2 (⅜″) wiggly eyes
Round oatmeal box with lid (18-ounce size)
Craft knife
1 yard of 1″-wide green ribbon
Rubber band

1. Trace and cut out all patterns. From pink paper, cut 1 tail and 2 ears. From the black paper, cut 2 hearts for cheeks and 4 triangles for toes.

2. To make the nose, cut off 1″ from the paper towel tube. Trace the nose pattern on pink paper and cut it out. Stand the tube in the middle of the nose circle and draw around it. With the scissors, make a cut from the outside of the circle to the pencil line. Make about 6 cuts, spacing them around the circle. Put glue on the cut edges. Place the circle over 1 end of the tube and glue the edges down. Cut a 1″ x 5½″ strip from the pink paper and glue it around the nose tube. For nostrils, use the hole punch to make 2 circles from black paper and glue them in the center of the nose.

3. To make the head, trace 1 head on the poster board. Cut it out just inside the pencil line. Then trace 2 heads on pink paper. Cut them out a little bit outside pencil line. Glue 1 pink head to 1 side of the poster board head. Let the glue dry.

4. To make the face, glue on 2 heart cheeks. With the black marker draw a smile connecting the hearts. Glue the nose to the face. Glue on wiggly eyes just above the nose.

5. Curl the 2 ears using the blade of the scissors. Then glue the bottoms of the ears to the back of the poster board head (ears should curl forward). Glue the other pink paper head to the back of the poster board, covering the bottoms of the ears.

Level 3

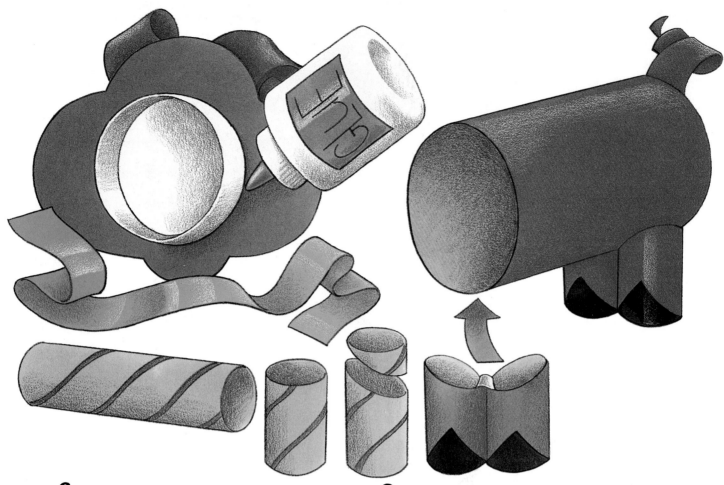

6. Take off the lid of the oatmeal box. Trim the rim of the lid so that it is only ½″ wide. Center Pig E.'s head on the top of the lid and glue it in place. Let it dry. Beginning under the chin, glue the ribbon around the neck. Cut off the extra ribbon and tie it in a bow. Glue the bow under the chin covering the ends of the other ribbon.

7. To make the body, cut out the bottom circle pattern. Trace it on pink paper and cut it out. Stand the oatmeal box in the center of the circle and draw around it. With scissors, cut to the pencil line, just as you did for the nose. Put glue on the circle and the edges. Glue the circle to the bottom of the box and the edges to the sides of the box. Cut a rectangle 5¼″ x 10½″ and glue it around the sides of the box. Curl the tail with the blade of the scissors and glue it in place. Ask your Mom or Dad to use a craft knife and cut a 1¼″ slit in the center of Pig E.'s back for coins.

8. To make the legs, cut 4 (2″) lengths from the wrapping paper tube. Cut off ⅜″ from the top inside half of each leg. (Then the top of the legs will be angled, making it easier for Pig E.'s body to sit on them.) Cut out the foot circle pattern. Trace it 4 times on pink paper and cut the circles out. Stand a leg in the center of each circle and draw around it. Cut and glue the foot, just as you did the nose. Repeat for the other legs. Cut 4 pink paper strips 2″ x 4½″ . Glue around each leg. Glue 1 toe triangle to the center front of each leg. Use rubber bands to hold them in place until they dry.

Trim the paper on the inside top of each leg to match the shape of the tube. Tape the tops of 2 legs together on the shorter sides. Tape the other 2 in the same way. Then glue them to Pig E.'s tummy, 1 pair in the front and 1 pair in the back.

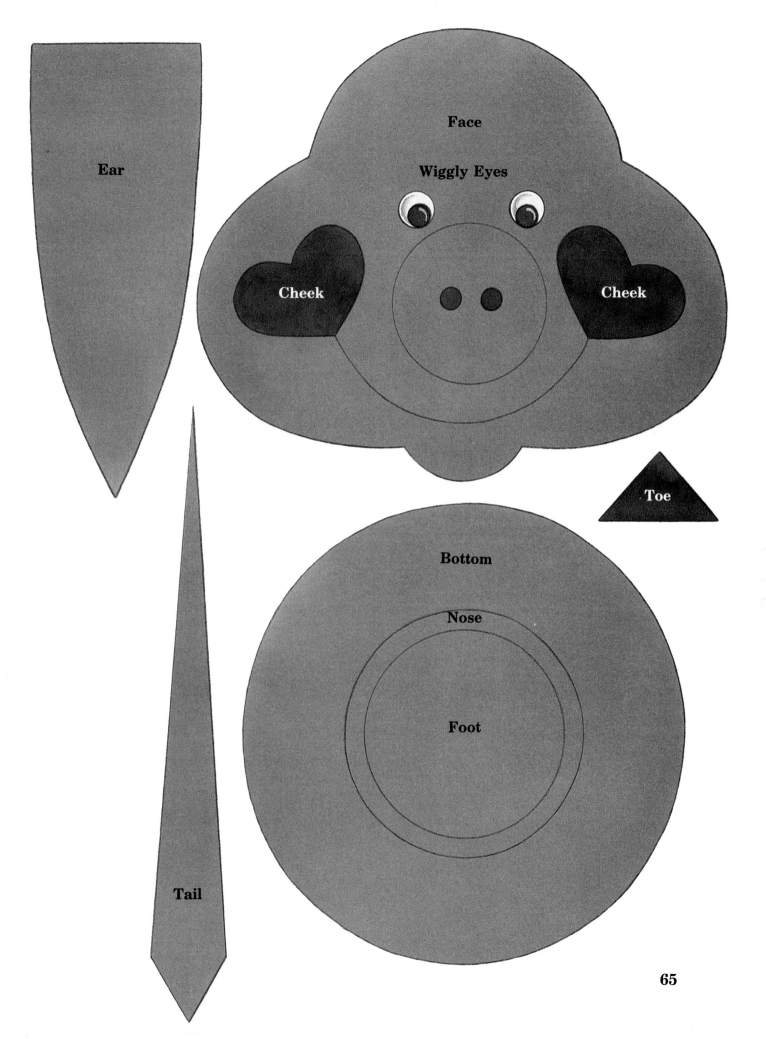

Ear

Face

Wiggly Eyes

Cheek

Cheek

Toe

Bottom

Nose

Foot

Tail

65

Balloon Bow

Brightly colored balloons make this barrette extra-special. And it's so easy to make, you'll want to make some in lots of different colors for lots of different friends.

You will need (for 1 barrette):
French-clasp barrette
Covered wire
20 to 25 (3″) balloons
Scissors

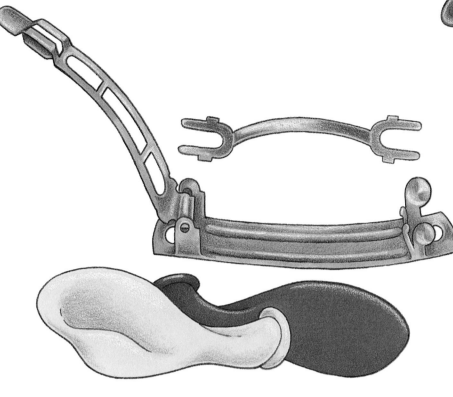

1. Open the barrette and fold back the clasp. To make attaching the balloons easier, remove the center bar and set it aside.

2. Hold the barrette upright and wrap the wire securely around 1 end.

3. Starting at the end of the barrette where the wire is attached, place 2 balloons on the barrette. Wrap the wire around the middle of the balloons to hold them to the barrette.

4. Holding the first 2 balloons out of the way, wire 2 more ballons right next to them. Continue wiring on balloons this way until the barrette is covered.

5. When the last 2 balloons are attached, wrap the wire around the other end of the barrette and cut away any extra wire. Replace the center bar in the barrette.

Level 2

Baseball Card Bag

You're sure to score a home run when you give this gift to a friend who collects baseball cards.

You will need:
Pencil
Soft drink can
Scrap of white felt
Fabric glue
2 (5½" x 7½") pieces of light blue-striped fabric
Red slick paint
Needle and thread
4 (½") plastic rings
Decorative shoelace

1. To make the baseball, set the drink can on the felt and trace around it. Cut out the circle.

2. Using the photograph as a guide, draw the lines for the stitching pattern on the baseball. Trace over the lines with the red slick paint. Let the paint dry.

3. Glue the ball in place on the right side of 1 piece of fabric. Let it dry.

4. With a pencil, write the word Baseball above the baseball and Cards below the baseball. Trace over the words with the slick paint. Let them dry.

5. Ask a grown-up to sew the bag together. With right sides facing, stitch the bag front and back together along the sides and bottom, leaving the top open. Turn the bag right side out and press it. Press under ¼″ along the top edge and stitch it in place.

6. On the outside of the bag, sew 1 ring at each side seam, 1 at the center front, and 1 at the center back, 1″ from the top.

7. Thread the shoelace through the rings, beginning and ending at 1 side seam. Knot both ends of the lace. Fill the bag with baseball cards. Draw up the shoelace and tie it in a knot to close the bag.

Safety Pin Bracelets

Add buttons and beads to safety pins and what do you have? One-of-a-kind jewelry for Mom. It's fun to make and really looks great!

Button Bracelets

You will need:
75 to 100 safety pins
100 (⅜″) buttons
200 beads (optional)
⅓ yard of elastic cord

1. On each safety pin slip 1 bead, 1 button, and 1 more bead or slip on just 1 button as shown on the purple bracelet.

2. Measure the wrist of the person who is to receive this bracelet. Add 1″ to that measurement and cut 1 piece of cord equal to the total measurement. Tie a knot in 1 end of the cord big enough to hold the pins on the cord.

3. Thread the pins onto the cord, threading the first pin through the hole in the clasp, the next through the hole in the bottom, and so on. Stop 1″ from the end.

4. Untie the knot at the other end of the cord. Then tie both ends of the cord together in a knot.

70 *Level 2*

Pearl Bracelet

You will need:
75 to 100 safety pins
300 pearl beads
500 colored beads
½ yard of elastic cord

1. Separate the safety pins into 2 equal piles. On the pins in 1 pile, slip colored beads only. Now separate the remaining safety pins into 2 equal piles. On the pins in 1 pile, slip 1 pearl, 2 beads, and 1 pearl. Then on the pins in the second pile, slip 2 beads, 1 pearl, and 2 beads.

2. Measure the wrist of the person who is to receive the bracelet. Add 1″ to the measurement. Cut 2 pieces of elastic cord, each equal to the total measurement. Tie a knot in 1 end of each cord big enough to hold the pins on the cord.

3. Start with a pin with just beads. (Since there are more of these, use them between the other pins.) Thread the end of 1 cord through the hole in the clasp. Thread the end of the other cord through the hole at the bottom of the pin. Now take a pin with 2 beads and 2 pearls and turn it upside-down. Thread the cords through the holes. Next, turn a pin with just beads right side up and thread it onto the cords. Now thread a pin with 1 pearl (upside-down) onto the cords. If you continue adding pins in this way, you will make a pretty pattern. Or you can make up your own pattern.

4. When you are 1″ from the end of the cords, stop adding pins. Untie the knots and tie the ends of each cord together.

71

Paw Pad

Make this place mat for your pet, and he'll know right where to stand when you serve his Christmas chow.

You will need:
18″ x 12″ blue foam-backed vinyl
Ruler
Pencil
Scissors
Tracing paper
Tape
White colored pencil
Paintbrush
   Acrylic paints: white, black
      Newspapers
      Clear acrylic spray

Level 1

1. Using the ruler, draw a line across each corner of the rectangle. Cut off the corners.

2. Trace and cut out the pattern pieces for the knife, fork, and spoon. Choose the size paw pattern that fits your pet. Trace and cut it out. (It's the left paw.) Now turn the pattern over to trace the right paw.

3. Arrange the pattern pieces on the vinyl. When the arrangement looks right, tape the pattern pieces in place so that they won't move while you're tracing them. Trace each pattern piece with the white pencil.

4. Remove the patterns. Using the paintbrush, paint the fork, knife, and spoon with white paint. Let the paint dry. Then paint a second coat.

5. Paint the paws with black paint. Let them dry. Then paint a second coat.

6. Let the place mat dry overnight. With a clean cloth, carefully wipe off any pencil marks that show. Be careful not to wipe off any paint.

7. In a well-ventilated room, lay the place mat on newspaper and spray it lightly with the clear acrylic spray. Spray on 4 more very light coats, letting the place mat dry between coats. This will help keep the paint from getting scratched off by your pet's claws.

Clear Acrylic Spray

Left Paw

Left Paw

Left Paw

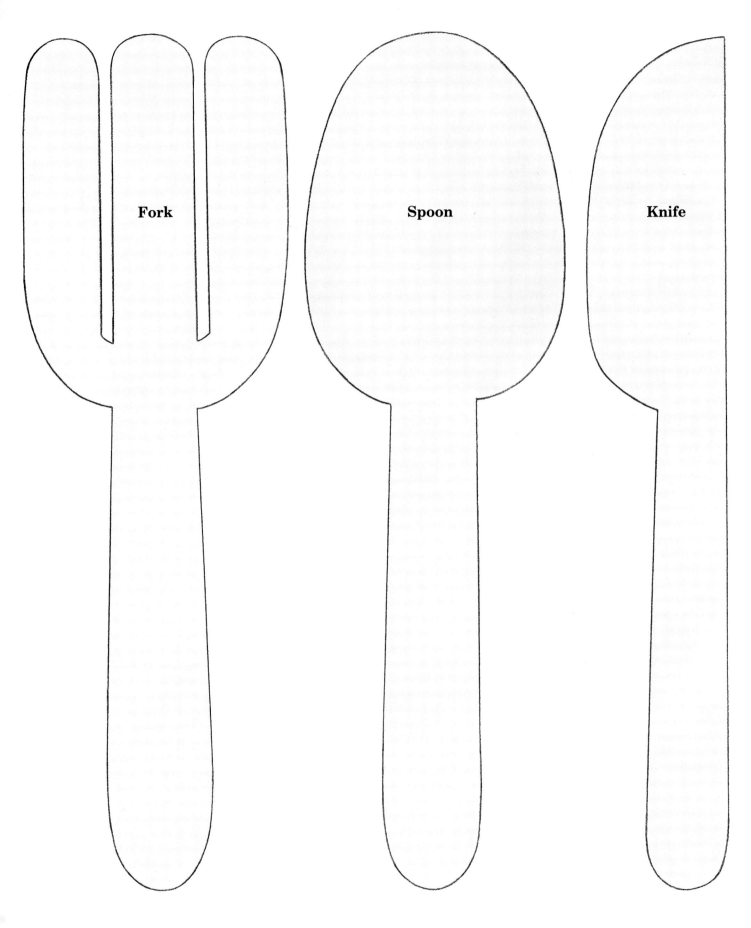

Fork

Spoon

Knife

74

Family Tree

Lots of people are interested in genealogy today. That's the history of a family. And one way to help organize information about a family is to make a family tree. The family tree tells who the parents or grandparents are and gives the names of all their children. This family tree is very simple—with just Mom, Dad, and the kids. But you could make a larger tree and put your grandparents or even your great-grandparents at the top.

You will need:
Tracing paper
Pencil
Scissors
Black fine-tip marker
Kitchen sponge
Paintbrush
Tempera paint: red, brown
9″ x 11″ piece of white construction paper
Green stamp pad

1. Trace and cut out the patterns.

2. Use the marker to trace around the tree and apple patterns on the sponge. Cut out the shapes with scissors.

3. Use the paintbrush to paint 1 side of the tree trunk sponge brown. Press the painted side of the sponge in the center of the white construction paper, with the bottom of the trunk about 1″ from the bottom of the paper.

4. Paint 1 side of the apple sponge red. Make a sponge-print apple for each member of the family, starting near the top of the tree with Mom and Dad. (See the photograph.) You may need to repaint your apple sponge between apples.

5. When the paint is dry, print a name beside each apple. After labeling an apple for Mom and an apple for Dad add the children's names according to age. Put the oldest child's name near the next highest apple on the tree. Write the name of the youngest child near the apple closest to the ground.

6. To make the leaves, press your index finger onto the green stamp pad. Then use your inked finger to make fingerprint leaves. Make as many leaves as you want. Re-ink your fingertip if the leaves get too light. To make the darker leaves, ink your finger on the pad again and make a second fingerprint leaf on top of the first.

7. When the ink is dry, use the marker to draw stems on the apples, and outline leaves that are near the stems. (See the photograph.) Print your family name neatly across the tree trunk near the base of the tree. Center and print "My Family Tree" below the tree.

Apple

Tree Trunk

Funky Frames

With buttons and bows and all kinds of little mementos, you can make a one-of-a-kind gift for a special friend.

You will need:
Ribbon
Scissors
White glue
Acrylic frame
Colorful buttons, paper clips, charms,
  erasers, and other small items

1. Cut pieces of ribbon and glue them along the edges of the frame. Make a bow and glue it to a top corner of the frame. Let the glue dry.

2. Glue the other things around the frame. Let the glue dry.

Hints:

• Choose a photograph and put it inside the frame before decorating.
• Use colorful trinkets.
• The bigger the frame, the crazier you can make it.
• Coordinate the colors with your friend's room.
• Use red and green ribbons and mementos for a Christmassy frame.

Parents' Workshop
Great Gifts for Children

Smocked Christmas Packages

You can keep these gifts under wraps all through the holidays and beyond. The smocked design was created as an insert for a Christmas outfit, but change the colors on the packages and it could just as easily be used for a special birthday suit.

You will need:

5½" x 45" piece of white broadcloth fabric, pleated with 12 gathering rows for smocking

Embroidery floss: red, kelly green, chartreuse, yellow, white

Large-eyed #10 crewel needle

Note: All smocking, ribbons, and bows are worked with 4 strands of floss unless otherwise noted.

1. For the borders, stitch continuous cable rows across gathering rows 1 and 10, using 4 strands of red floss.

2. Begin smocking the first package on the left. Start with an up cable on row 9, 11 pleats from the left, as indicated by the arrow on the diagram. Cable 35 green for the first row of the package, turn work, and cable 35 green back across. Continue working to complete 14 rows of cable. Begin each package with the cable

in the lower left corner and stack the stitches upward. Finish each package before beginning the next. FOLLOW DIAGRAM CAREFULLY FOR CABLE COUNT AND PLACEMENT.

3. On the wrong side of the fabric, backsmock across rows 2 and 3 with 2 strands of white floss. Use a cable row the same length as your borders. On remaining rows, backsmock across all unsmocked areas to hold pleats in place.

4. For the ribbons, work straight stitches over the smocked packages as shown. For the bows, make lazy daisy loops centered with French knots (wrap needle twice). For the ends of the bows, make straight stitches that are very loose and curve (see diagram). To secure the bows and ribbons, take several tiny stitches, using 1 strand of floss, to hold the long stitches in place.

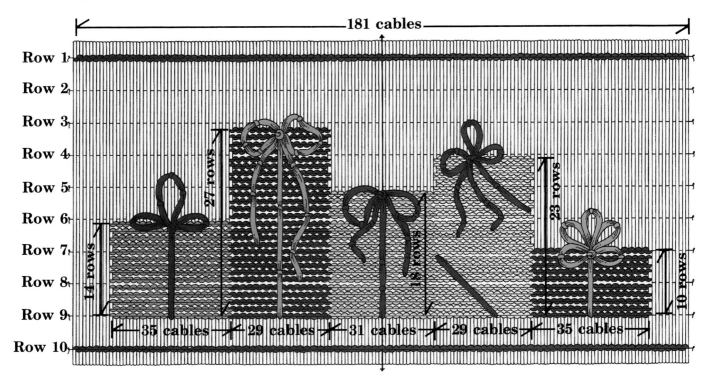

Walk on the Wild Side

Lions and tigers and monkeys, oh my! These wild designs probably won't tame your wild animals, but whether they're two or 12, kids will roar with pleasure when wearing these stenciled shirts.

You will need:
Tracing paper
Artist's spray adhesive
Acetate
Craft knife
Cardboard square
Shirt
Black fabric paint
Sponge

1. Fold the tracing paper in half and crease it. Unfold the paper and lay the creased edge on the fold line of the stencil pattern. Trace the design, shading all dark areas. To complete the animal face pattern, fold the untraced half of the tissue over the traced half and trace over the first tracing.

2. Unfold the pattern, spray it with adhesive, and apply to the acetate.

3. Cut out the dark areas in the design, using the craft knife.

4. Inside the shirt, place a piece of cardboard that is large enough to stretch the front slightly. (This will give you a smooth surface on which to apply the stencil and to paint.) Remove the tracing paper from the acetate stencil. Lightly spray the stencil with adhesive and apply it to the center front of the shirt.

5. Pour the fabric paint into a bowl. Using a sponge, apply the paint to the shirt in an up-and-down motion over the stencil. All cut out areas will be black. (Do not remove stencil yet.) Let the paint dry according to the manufacturer's directions. If the design is not dark enough, apply a second coat of paint. Remove the stencil when the paint is dry.

Lion

After completing pattern, add mane lines where desired. (See photo.)

Mane lines

Zebra

Place on fold.

Place on fold.

Monkey

Tiger

Place on fold.

88

Holly Days Skirt & Sweater

This simple sewing and cross-stitch project makes it easy for even the busiest of mothers to make a special holiday outfit for her little girl. Add the holly design to a purchased sweater, stitch the simple skirt, and her holly-days wardrobe is complete.

Skirt

You will need:
Red gingham (¹⁄₁₆″ check) fabric (for
  amount, see Step 1)
1 yard (¾″-wide) elastic
2 (¾″) buttons
White thread
DMC embroidery floss: 912, 911, 909, 321
Embroidery needle
Purchased red sweater

Note: Use ½″ seam allowances through-
out project unless instructed otherwise.

1. To figure the amount of fabric needed
for the skirt, add 8″ to the desired fin-
ished length. Cut out 2 pieces this total
length, each piece 36″ wide, or twice the
child's waist measurement, whichever is
less. The remaining fabric will be used for
the suspenders.

2. With right sides facing, sew the skirt
pieces together at the sides.

3. For the waistband, press under ¼″
along the top edge of the skirt. Then
press under 2″ more. On the wrong side,

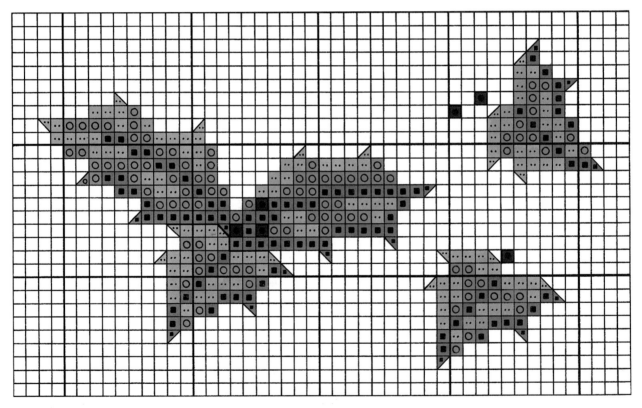

Stitch Count (for cross-stitch design):
45 x 25
**Stitch Count (for duplicate-stitch
design): 31 x 19**

Color Code

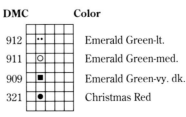

DMC		Color
912	··	Emerald Green-lt.
911	○	Emerald Green-med.
909	■	Emerald Green-vy. dk.
321	●	Christmas Red

90

machine-stitch the waistband leaving a 1″ opening. To make a casing for the elastic, stitch again, 1″ above the first stitching.

4. Cut a piece of elastic the length of the waist measurement plus 1½″. Attach a large safety pin to 1 end. Insert the elastic through the opening in the casing, leaving 1″ on each end outside the casing. Remove the safety pin and overlap and stitch the ends of the elastic together. Let the elastic slip inside the casing. Stitch the opening closed.

5. To figure the fabric needed for the suspenders, measure from the front waistline straight up to the shoulder, diagonally across the back, and down to the back waistline. Add 5″ to this length. Cut 4 strips this total length and 2½″-wide. With right sides facing and raw edges aligned, sew 2 strips together along both sides and across 1 end. Repeat for the other suspender. Turn both suspenders right side out. Slipstitch the open end closed. Press. Topstitch along all edges.

6. Inside the front waistband, tack 1 end of each suspender where desired along the casing. (Each suspender should be the same distance from the side seams.) Center and sew a button to the outside of the skirt through 1 suspender and the elastic. Repeat with the second button. Cross the suspenders in the back and hand-stitch in place inside the back waistband, again making sure they are an equal distance from the side seams and adjusting for proper skirt length.

7. Press under ¼″ along the bottom edge of the skirt. Press under 3″ more and hem.

Cross-stitching Skirt

1. Use 3 strands of DMC floss. Stitch over 9 squares (3 checks x 3 checks) of the gingham for each cross-stitch.

2. Begin stitching the design in the center front of the skirt, alternating the large holly motif and the 2 holly leaves. Repeat the design on the back of the skirt.

Duplicate-stitching Sweater

1. Use the graph of the large holly motif as a guide for duplicate-stitching the sweater. (Figure A and Figure B.) Use 6 strands of DMC floss.

2. Begin stitching the design on the center front, 1 row from the center ribbing on each side. Space the design evenly around the sweater.

Duplicate Stitch

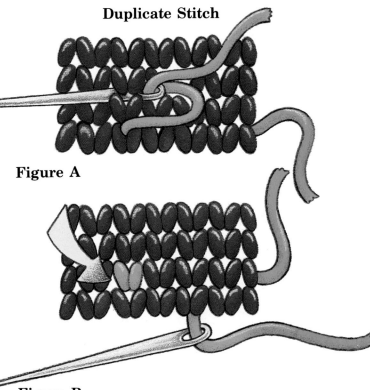

Figure A

Figure B

Stars & Bars Sweater

This star-studded sweater, knitted in a washable cotton yarn, will keep young stargazers comfortable while dreaming of faraway galaxies.

You will need:
Sizes 4 and 6 knitting needles (or size to obtain gauge)
Sportweight cotton yarn (50-gram skeins): 3 skeins blue, 2 skeins red, 2 skeins yellow, 1 skein green
Bobbins (optional)
Stitch holder
Size 4 (16″) circular knitting needle
Tapestry needle

Standard Knitting Abbreviations

st(s)—stitch(es)
St st—stockinette stitch
k—knit
p—purl
beg—begin(ning)
rem—remain(ing)
dec—decrease(s)
inc—increase(s)

Sizing chart	S	M	L
Chest (actual size)	23″	24″	26″
Chest (finished size)	26″	27″	29″
Length (shoulder to hip)	16″	17″	17½″
Sleeve length	10½″	11½″	12½″

Gauge: 5 sts and 7 rows = 1″ in St st on larger needles.

Note: Since it is best not to carry yarn over more than 2 stitches, it may be easier to wind yarn on bobbins while working the graph. To avoid holes, twist old yarn over new when changing colors. Directions are given for size small. Changes for sizes medium and large are given in parentheses. (See graph on page 94.)

Back: With smaller needles and blue, cast on 64 (68, 72) sts. Work in k 1, p 1 ribbing for 2″ (3″, 3½″). Change to larger needles and work in St st until piece measures 16″ (17″, 17½″) from beg. Bind off loosely.

Front: Cast on sts and work ribbing as for back. Change to larger needles and work in St st according to graph. Be sure to follow graph for appropriate size. Shape neckline as indicated on graph, working both shoulders at the same time, using separate yarn. Following graph, work across 24 (26, 28) sts, slip center 16 sts to a stitch holder, attach new yarn and work across rem 24 (26, 28) sts. Continuing to work in St st and following graph, dec 1 st each side of neck edge every other row, 7 times. When graph is completed, front should measure same as back. Bind off all shoulder sts loosely.

Sleeves: Work 1 in red and 1 in yellow. With smaller needles, cast on 38 (40, 42) sts. Work in k 1, p 1 ribbing for 2″. Change to larger needles and inc 8 sts evenly spaced across first row of St st. Inc 1 st on each edge of sleeve, every 6th row, until 64 (68, 72) sts are on needle. Work even until sleeve measures 10½″ (11½″, 12½″) from beg. Bind off loosely. Repeat for second sleeve.

To finish: Using tapestry needle and blue, weave shoulder seams. For neck, with circular needle and green, pick up 76 (76, 80) sts. Work in k 1, p 1 ribbing for 1″. Bind off loosely in rib pattern.

To attach sleeves, measure down side seams from shoulder 6¼″ (6½″, 7¼″) and mark this point on front and back of sweater. Match center top of sleeve to shoulder seam and pin. Weave sleeve to sweater from point marked on front to point marked on back. Weave sleeve from wrist to underarm. Weave side seam from waist to underarm.

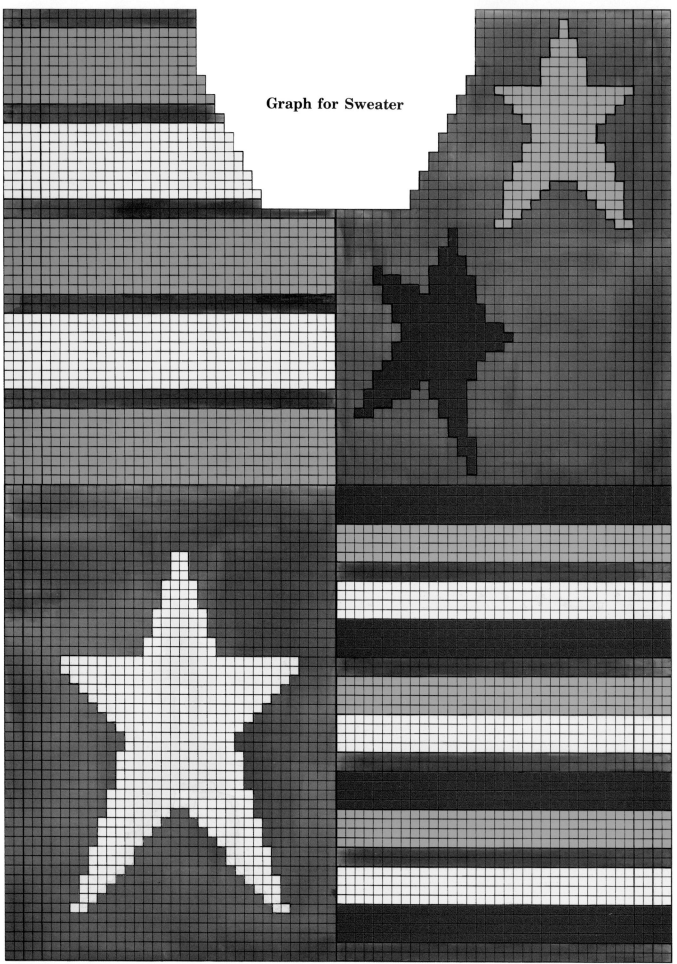

Graph for Sweater

L M S

S M L

Winter Sweats

Even if the weather outside is frightful, your kids will still look delightful in these adorable appliquéd sweatshirts.

Snow Bunny Sweatshirt

You will need:

Lightweight paper
Paper-backed fusible web
7" x 9" piece of medium-weight white
   fabric
4" square of orange fabric
Thread to match fabrics
Sweatshirt
½ yard (⅛"-wide) light green ribbon
Liquid ravel preventer
¼ yard (⅝"-wide) yellow ribbon
4 (½") white pom-poms
Embroidery floss: peach, black
Embroidery needle

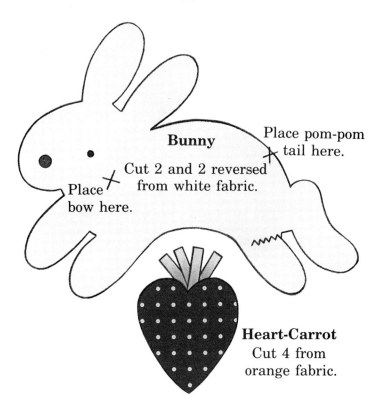

Bunny
Cut 2 and 2 reversed
from white fabric.

Place
bow here.

Place pom-pom
tail here.

Heart-Carrot
Cut 4 from
orange fabric.

1. Trace the bunny and heart-carrot patterns onto lightweight paper. Cut out. Fuse the web to the wrong side of the appliqué fabrics, according to the manufacturer's directions. Trace the patterns on the paper side of the web. Trace 4 carrots and 4 bunnies, with 2 bunnies facing right and 2 facing left. Cut out.

2. Cut 16 (¾") pieces of green ribbon. Divide them into 4 bunches of 4 each. Coat the ends with ravel preventer.

3. Arrange the bunnies on the sweatshirt. Remove the paper backing and fuse them to the sweatshirt. Place a green ribbon bunch under the top of each carrot, fanning the ends out at the top. Fuse the carrots to the sweatshirt.

4. Place lightweight paper under the front of the sweatshirt and machine-appliqué the motifs to the sweatshirt. For bunnies: Machine-appliqué around the hind leg first, then the body. When stitching is complete, tear away the paper from the back of the sweatshirt. Press.

5. Cut 4 (1") pieces of yellow ribbon. Coat the ends of the ribbons with ravel preventer. With needle and thread, run a gathering stitch across the center of each ribbon. Pull the gathering thread to make a bow. Then tightly wrap the thread around the center of the bow several times. Stitch through the center to secure. Sew a ribbon bow on each bunny's neck. Sew a white pom-pom tail on each bunny. Embroider each bunny's face, using 2 strands of embroidery floss. Satin-stitch the nose peach and make a black French knot for the eye.

Snowman Sweatshirt

You will need:

Lightweight paper
⅛ yard (36″-wide) red-and-white striped fabric
⅛ yard (36″-wide) green fabric
6″ x 9″ piece of red print fabric
5″ x 7″ piece of medium-weight white fabric
3″ x 4″ piece of black fabric
½ yard paper-backed fusible web
Sweatshirt
¼ yard (⅛″-wide) black ribbon
¼ yard (⅛″-wide) white ribbon
½ yard (1/16″-wide) white ribbon
¼ yard (½″-wide) decorative white ribbon
Liquid ravel preventer
Embroidery floss: pink, orange, and black
Embroidery needle
Tapestry needle
5″ x 7″ piece of clear plastic

Note: Use ¼″ seam allowances throughout the project.

1. To figure the length required for the decorative insert, measure across the front of the sweatshirt and add ½″. From the striped fabric, cut 1 strip 3½″ x the length of the insert. From the green fabric, cut 2 strips 1¼″ x the length of the insert. Fold the green strips in half, wrong sides facing and long edges aligned. Press. With right sides facing and raw edges aligned, sew 1 folded green strip to each long edge of the striped insert. Press the seam allowances toward the insert. Press under ¼″ on both ends of the insert.

2. Trace the appliqué patterns onto lightweight paper. Cut out. Fuse web to the wrong sides of the appliqué fabrics, according to the manufacturer's directions. Trace the patterns, face down, onto the paper side of the web. Cut out.

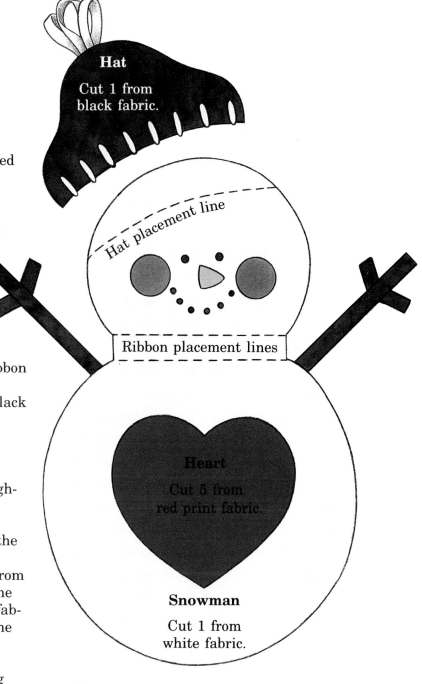

Hat
Cut 1 from black fabric.

Hat placement line

Ribbon placement lines

Heart
Cut 5 from red print fabric.

Snowman
Cut 1 from white fabric.

3. Pin the snowman appliqué piece in the center of the insert (do not fuse). Position 2 hearts on each side of the snowman as shown. Remove the snowman. Remove the paper backing from each of the 4 hearts. Fuse them in place on the insert. Before stitching, slide a piece of lightweight paper under the insert for stability. Then machine-appliqué the hearts, stitching through the paper. Stitch again for a smoother edge. Tear away the paper and press.

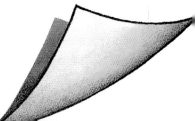

pin the 1″ ribbons across the arms ½″ from the ends. Remove the pins in the snowman and fuse him in place.

6. Cut a 6″ piece of (⅛″-wide) white ribbon. Fold it to form 3 loops and tack 1 end of the loops together. Remove the paper backing from the hat. Place the tacked end of the ribbon under the hat and fuse the hat to the sweatshirt.

7. Place lightweight paper under the sweatshirt front and machine-appliqué the design in place. Stitch again for a smoother edge. Straight-stitch the ribbon arms and hands in place. Tear away the paper and press.

8. Cut a 2½″ piece and 2 (1¼″) pieces of ½″-wide ribbon. Turn the ends of the 2½″ piece under to fit across the snowman's neck. Fuse a piece of web to the wrong side of the 2½″ ribbon. Position it across the snowman's neck. Place the 1¼″ pieces under the neck ribbon as shown. Remove the paper backing and fuse the neck ribbon. Straight-stitch along all sides of the neck ribbon, close to the edge. Do not stitch around the 1¼″ pieces. Put ravel preventer on the ribbon ends.

9. Embroider the snowman's face, using 2 strands of embroidery floss. Satin-stitch the cheeks pink and the nose orange. Add black French knots for the eyes and mouth. Thread a tapestry needle with the ¹⁄₁₆″-wide white ribbon. Knot 1 end. Stitch the decorative lines along the bottom of the snowman's hat as shown.

Using the appliqué pattern, cut one snowman from clear plastic. Trim the plastic away along the bottom of the hat. Hand-stitch the plastic over the snowman, just inside zigzag stitching.

4. Cut a piece of fusible web 3″ x the length of the insert. Fuse the web to the wrong side of the striped fabric, leaving the green strips free. Remove the paper backing. Position the insert on the sweatshirt front and fuse it in place. Then stitch the insert in place, sewing in the ditch (on the seam line) between the striped fabric and the green fabric. (Do not sew the outside edge of the green strip down.) Repeat along the bottom edge of the insert. Stitch the ends of the insert to the shirt, stitching close to the edge of the insert.

5. Remove the paper backing from the remaining heart. Fuse it to the snowman as shown. Remove the paper backing from the snowman. Pin the snowman in place on the sweatshirt as shown. Cut 2 (2″) pieces of black ribbon and 2 (1″) pieces. Pin 1 end of each 2″ ribbon under the snowman to form arms. To make hands,

P. J. Pooch

It's a no-sew appliqué! So quick, it won't take you a day. It's simple to add a special touch this way.

You will need:
Lightweight paper
⅓ yard of paper-backed fusible web
8″ square of white fleece
12″ x 6″ piece of black-and-white houndstooth fabric for pj's
Scraps of yellow, black, white, and red-and-white striped fabric
Red flannel nightshirt
17″ cardboard square
Tubes of fabric paint: white, yellow, black
Scissors
White pom-pom
White thread

1. Trace all the patterns onto light-weight paper and cut out.

2. Fuse the web to the wrong side of the appliqué fabrics, following the manufacturer's instructions. Then trace the patterns on the paper side of the fusible web. Cut out all the pieces as indicated.

3. Remove the paper backing from web on each appliqué piece before fusing in place. Using the photo as a guide, fuse the pj's on the nightshirt. Fuse the rest of P. J. Pooch in this order: bone, head, nose, hat, ear, tail. (See pattern for placement.) Using the photo as a guide, fuse the clouds and stars in place.

4. Insert the cardboard between the shirt front and back for a solid painting surface. With matching or coordinating paint colors, carefully outline all the fused shapes. Let dry. Referring to the pattern and working from upper left to lower right to avoid smearing, draw a black eye and outline pajama flap. Draw

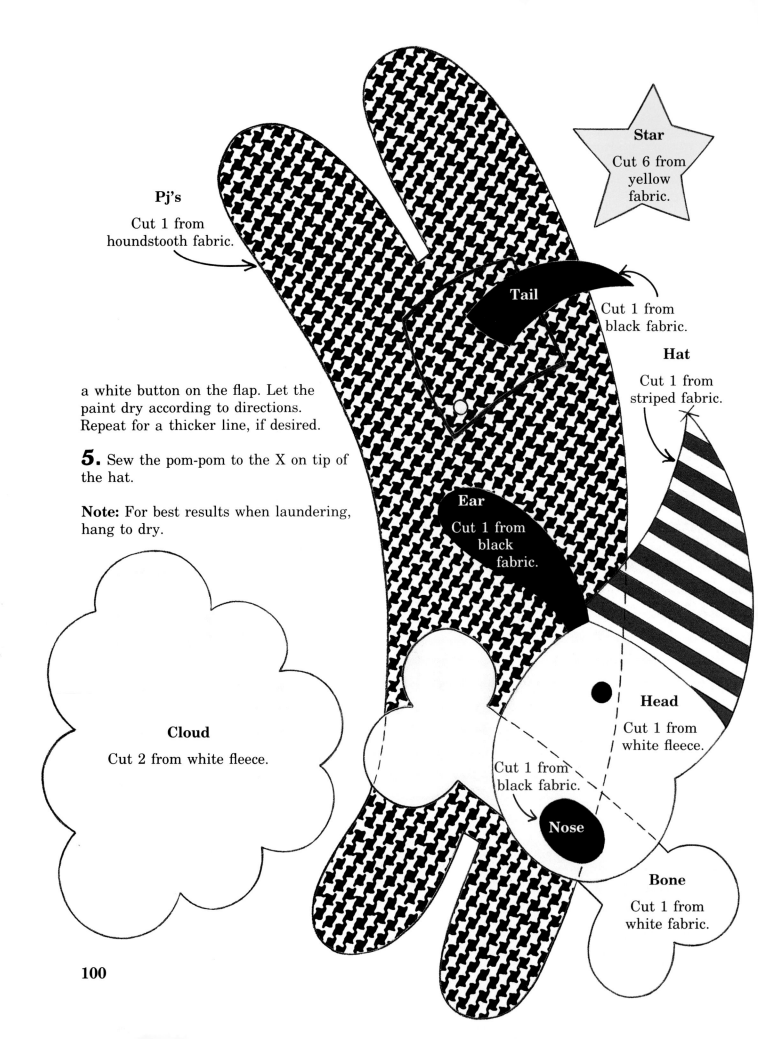

Star

Cut 6 from yellow fabric.

Pj's

Cut 1 from houndstooth fabric.

Tail

Cut 1 from black fabric.

Hat

Cut 1 from striped fabric.

a white button on the flap. Let the paint dry according to directions. Repeat for a thicker line, if desired.

5. Sew the pom-pom to the X on tip of the hat.

Note: For best results when laundering, hang to dry.

Ear
Cut 1 from black fabric.

Head

Cut 1 from white fleece.

Cut 1 from black fabric.

Nose

Cloud

Cut 2 from white fleece.

Bone

Cut 1 from white fabric.

Wagon Dragon

A few paint strokes, and imaginations will set sail, as this friendly dragon accompanies your little one on his rainy adventures.

You will need:
Child's yellow vinyl raincoat
Paper
¼″ paintbrush
White flat acrylic paint
Tubes of fabric paint: turquoise, bright
    blue, gray, red, bright yellow, white

1. Trace and transfer the design to the raincoat. Use the photo as a placement guide.

2. Undercoat the entire design with several coats of flat white paint. Let dry between coats. You may need to redraw some of the pattern lines if the undercoat covers them.

3. Using the pattern as a guide, apply the paint to the brush and paint the colors in the following order: turquoise, blue, gray, and red. Apply several coats of each color. Let dry between coats. The stars and sail will remain flat white.

4. When the paint is completely dry, outline and add the remaining design lines (see pattern) by squeezing paint directly from the tubes. Work from the top of the design to the bottom, being careful not to smear the paint. Be sure to let the paint dry at least 24 hours before wearing.

Wagon Dragon

103

Nativity Puzzle

Play the day away! That's what kids will do as they tell and retell the story of Christmas with this holiday puzzle. These sturdy puzzle pieces are just right for little hands. And the painted stable provides a background for imaginative minds at work.

You will need:
Tracing and graphite paper
12″ x 14½″ piece of 1″ pine shelving
12″ x 14½″ piece of ¼″ plywood
Jigsaw
Electric sander
Sandpaper (medium and fine grit)
Wood glue
Wood clamps
Enamel paints: red, blue, green, gray, yellow, flesh, white, black
Paintbrushes
Black paint marker
 Clear spray acrylic

1. Trace the patterns for the puzzle frame and pieces onto the tracing paper. Use the graphite paper to transfer the cutting lines and features from the tracing paper to the shelving.

2. Use the jigsaw to cut out the puzzle interior, inserting the saw where indicated on the pattern and exiting at the same point. Then cut each individual puzzle shape from this piece.

3. With the outside edges aligned, glue the remaining shelving to the plywood. Clamp together until the glue dries. Then cut along the outline of the stable, cutting through both layers.

4. Using the graphite paper, trace the stable background design onto the plywood backing.

5. Using the electric sander and medium-grit paper, sand the outside edges of the stable. By hand, sand the inside edges of the stable and each puzzle piece with fine-grit paper.

6. Paint the stable and the puzzle pieces as shown. Let dry. Then outline with the marker.

7. Spray each puzzle piece and the stable with 2 coats of acrylic, letting it dry between coats.

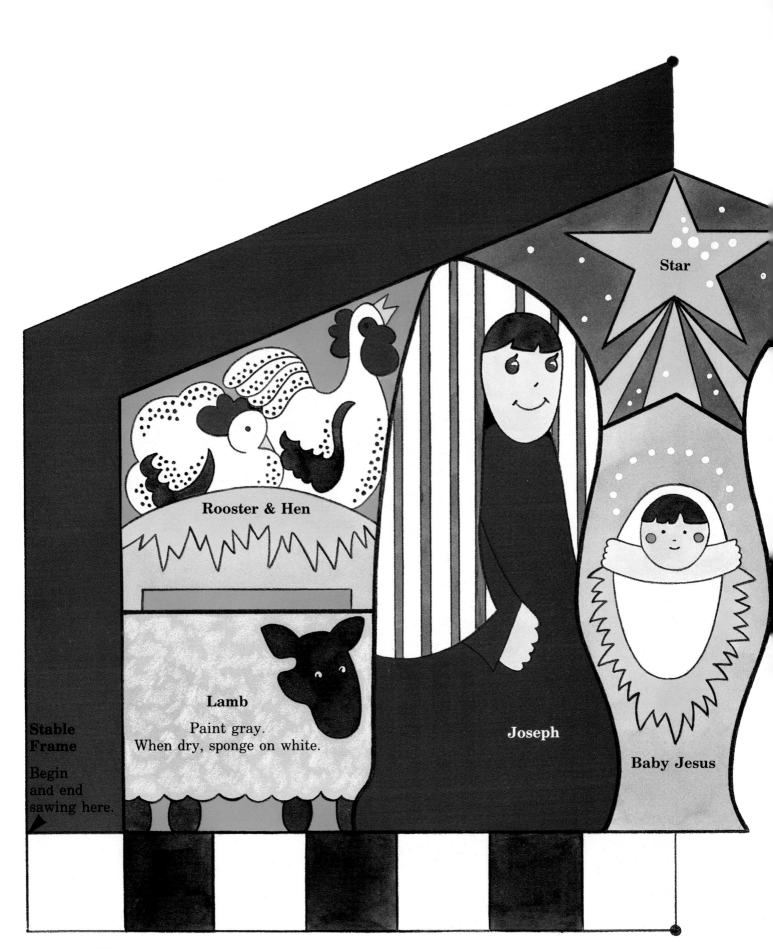

Star

Rooster & Hen

Lamb

Paint gray.
When dry, sponge on white.

Stable
Frame

Begin
and end
sawing here.

Joseph

Baby Jesus

106

Match dots and continue pattern across page.

Cow

Mary

Lamb
Paint gray.
When dry, sponge on white.

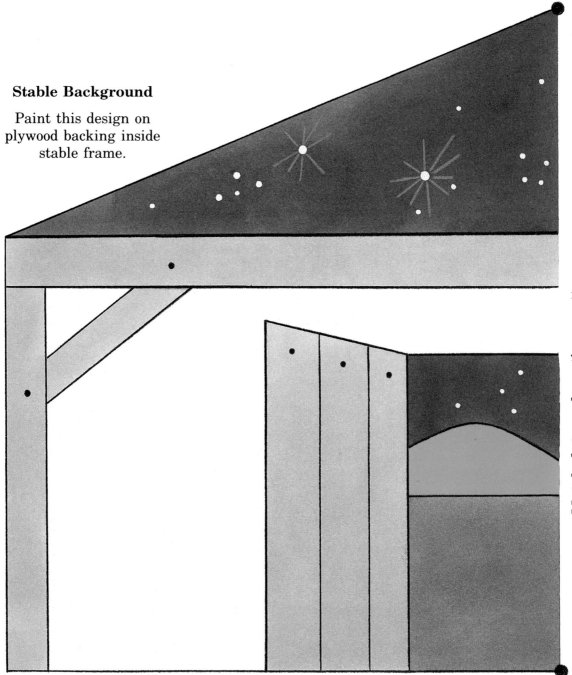

Stable Background

Paint this design on plywood backing inside stable frame.

Match dots and continue pattern across page.

109

Travel Tic-Tac-Toe

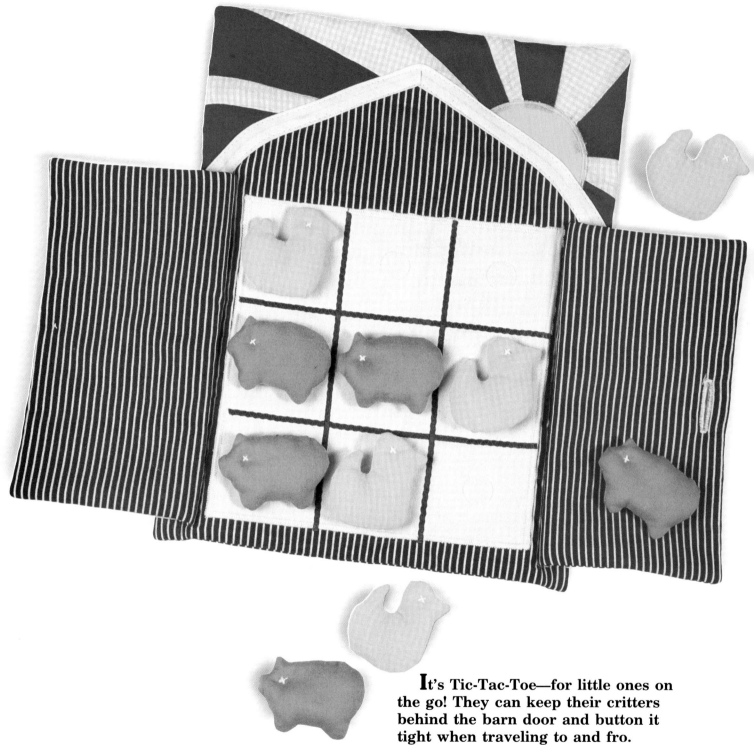

It's Tic-Tac-Toe—for little ones on the go! They can keep their critters behind the barn door and button it tight when traveling to and fro.

You will need:

1 (12″ x 16″) piece each of yellow, blue, hot pink, and yellow-checked cotton fabrics
⅓ yard (45″-wide) red-and-white striped fabric
⅔ yard (36″-wide) quilt batting
7″ square of white fabric
10″ x 12½″ piece of muslin
⅞ yard (⅛″-wide) blue satin ribbon
White and transparent nylon thread
2 yards (½″-wide) white bias tape
Hot-glue gun and glue stick
⅝″ flat white button
Polyester stuffing
White embroidery floss
10 (½″) Velcro dots

Note: Add ¼″ seam allowances to all pieces except sun and white square.

1. Trace all the patterns. Cut pieces from fabrics as marked.

2. From the red-and-white striped fabric, cut 1 (10″ x 12½″) rectangle for the backing and 4 (5″ x 8″) rectangles for the doors. From the quilt batting, cut 1 (10″ x 12½″) rectangle and 2 (5″ x 8″) rectangles. Cut a 7″ square from white fabric.

3. Using the pattern as a guide, stitch the pieces of the sky and the sun's rays together, with right sides facing and raw edges aligned. Press seams open. With top edges aligned and right sides facing up, baste the sky/rays to the muslin. Baste sun in place, referring to the pattern for position.

4. Baste the barn front, right side up, to the muslin, aligning the bottom and side edges of the barn with the muslin. Pin the white fabric square ⅞″ from the bottom edge and 1⅜″ from the side edges of the barn front. Using white thread, machine-appliqué the square in place. With a pencil, divide the square into 9 equal sections. Cut 4 (7″) lengths of blue ribbon. Using transparent thread, zigzag the ribbon over the pencil lines. (See photo.)

5. Center the bias tape along the roof line of the barn. Stitch both edges of the tape in place.

6. Stack the pieces in this order: 10″ x 12½″ piece of quilt batting, appliquéd front (right side up), and backing (right side down). With raw edges aligned, stitch around the edges, leaving a 3″ opening. Clip and trim corners. Turn right side out and press; slipstitch the opening closed.

7. Using transparent thread, machine-appliqué the sun in place, stitching through all layers.

8. To make the barn doors, stack the pieces in this order: 1 (5″ x 8″) piece of quilt batting, 1 barn door (right side up), and 1 barn door (right side down). With raw edges aligned, stitch around the edges, leaving a 2″ opening. Clip and trim

Cow Clock

Hey, diddle diddle, there's no cat or fiddle, but there is a cow jumping over the moon. And stenciled on a wooden clock face, this Mother Goose character will keep time jumping in a young child's room.

You will need:

Tracing paper
Graphite paper
$\frac{3}{4}''$ x 12″ piece clear (no knots) pine
Saber saw or coping saw
Drill with $\frac{1}{16}''$ and $\frac{5}{16}''$ bits
Coarse sandpaper
Clockworks to fit through the clock face
Wood chisel
Hammer
Acrylic paints: clear, white, blue, yellow,
   black, red
Paintbrush
Clear plastic for stencils
Ballpoint pen
Craft knife
Masking tape
Stencil brushes and sponges
Fine-tip paintbrush
2 ($2\frac{1}{2}''$) wood screws
Acrylic spray

Cutting and Painting

1. Trace the outline of the clock face and base. Using graphite paper transfer the patterns to the wood and cut out.

2. Mark the center of the clock face and drill a hole through the clock with a $\frac{5}{16}''$ bit. Mark the holes on the base and the bottom of the clock. Drill, using a $\frac{1}{16}''$ bit. Using coarse sandpaper, sand all pieces, slightly rounding the edges of the clock face.

3. From the back of the clock, fit the shaft of the clockworks through the hole in the clock face, making sure the threads of the shaft clear the clock face.

Note: If threads don't clear the clock face, recess the works into the back of the clock, using the following procedure: With the shaft still inserted through the clock, trace the outline of the works box; remove the box. Using a sharp chisel and hammer,

tap $\frac{1}{8}''$ into the wood along the box outline. Chisel out the area inside the outline. Smooth the recessed area with the chisel.

4. For base coats, apply 3 coats of white paint to both the clock and the base, letting the paint dry between coats. When dry, paint the base white 1 more time. Paint the clock blue. Let dry.

Stenciling the Clock Face

Note: Read all directions before beginning. Stencil in the order given.

1. To make stencils, lay a piece of stencil plastic over each pattern. With a ballpoint pen, trace the pattern and any registration marks (marks on which to line up your stencil). Cut out stencils with a craft knife.

2. Lay the stencil on the area to be painted and tape it in place, lining up any registration marks. Apply paint sparingly with stencil brushes or sponges in an up-and-down motion. If a more solid coverage is desired, apply several coats before removing stencil. Be sure to allow time to dry between coats.

3. First, with the sponge, stencil the clouds white, with heavier coverage around edges. Then with the stencil brush, paint the numbers and dots black. Paint the moon and stars white. When they are dry, re-paint them yellow. Paint the cow body and ear black. Paint the face, brush of tail, hooves, and hearts with coats of white until desired intensity is reached. Paint the ribbon and bell white; then re-paint the ribbon red and the bell yellow. With the fine-tip brush, make a white dot for the eye. Let dry. Then make a black dot for the pupil and paint the nostril black.

Clock Face

Center Hole

Assembling the Clock

1. Insert the wood screws through the bottom of the base into the holes in bottom edge of the clock. Tighten screws, countersinking the screw heads.

2. Retouch any imperfections in stenciling and let dry. Apply several coats of spray acrylic, allowing it to dry between coats.

3. Follow the manufacturer's instructions to connect the clock works.

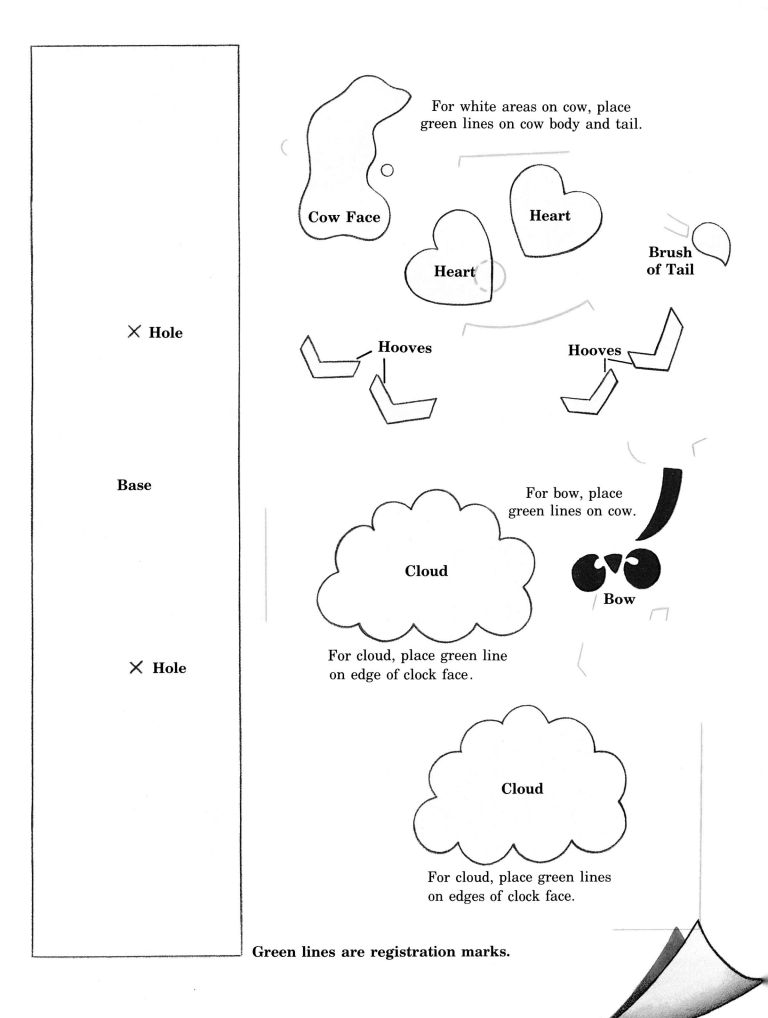

Hole

Base

Hole

Cow Face

For white areas on cow, place
green lines on cow body and tail.

Heart

Heart

**Brush
of Tail**

Hooves

Hooves

For bow, place
green lines on cow.

Cloud

Bow

For cloud, place green line
on edge of clock face.

Cloud

For cloud, place green lines
on edges of clock face.

Green lines are registration marks.

Ear

Cow Body

For cow, place green lines
on edges of moon.

Numbers and Dots

For bell, place green
lines on edges of bow.

Bell

Stars

For moon, place green lines
on edges of clouds.

Moon

118

Bedtime Caddy

All aboard! Storybooks, markers, and coloring books will ride the rails in style when they're stored in this bedtime caddy. Slip the unappliquéd section of the caddy between the mattress and boxsprings, and your little engineer will have everything at his fingertips.

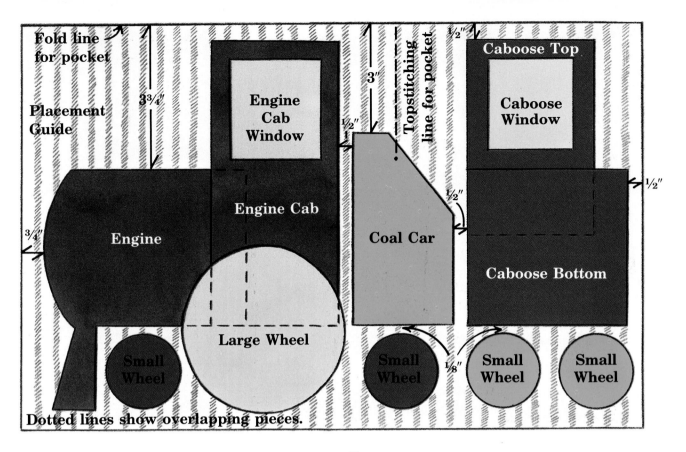

Dotted lines show overlapping pieces.

You will need:

¾ yard (45″-wide) navy pindot fabric
½ yard (45″-wide) polyester fleece
½ yard (45″-wide) striped ticking fabric
¼ yard each (45″-wide) red, gold, and
   green pindot fabrics
Thread to match fabrics
½ yard of fusible web
3 yards (1″-wide) red pindot double-fold
   bias tape

Note: Use ¼″ seam allowances through-out project unless instructed otherwise. Machine-appliqué all pieces using a medium-width zigzag or satin stitch and matching thread.

1. Cut a 17″ x 32″ rectangle from the navy pindot fabric and polyester fleece. Cut a 17″ x 22″ rectangle from the ticking fabric. Cut an 11″ x 17″ rectangle from the fusible web. To aid in appliquéing, fuse the web to the wrong side of the ticking fabric, aligning 1 (17″) edge of the web with 1 (17″) edge of the ticking fabric. (Appliqué shapes on this half of the ticking fabric.)

2. Transfer the patterns for the appliqué pieces and cut as marked.

3. With right sides facing, pin the large wheels together. Stitch, leaving an opening for turning. Clip seams and turn right side out. Slipstitch the opening closed. Press.

4. Fold the engine cab and the engine cab window along the fold lines, wrong sides facing. Press. Lay the cab with the folded side at the top. Referring to the diagram, pin the cab window to the cab, also with the folded side at the top. Appliqué around the window, leaving the top edge of the window unstitched. Appliqué the caboose window to the caboose top in the same way.

5. With wrong sides facing, fold the engine along the fold line and press. Referring to diagram, pin the engine on the ticking with the fold of the fabric at the top. Appliqué around the left and the bottom edges only, leaving the right edge and the fold unstitched. Pin the engine cab in place, overlapping 1″ of the engine's raw edge and aligning the bottom edge of the cab and engine. Appliqué, leaving the folded edge unstitched.

6. With right sides facing, stitch the coal car along the diagonal edge. Turn and press. Pin the coal car to the ticking, ½″ from the engine and with bottom edges of cars aligned. Appliqué, leaving the top and diagonal edges unstitched.

7. Press the caboose top and pin it ½″ from the coal car, aligning the top folded edge with the top edge of the engine. Appliqué, leaving both the top and the left edge unstitched.

  With wrong sides facing, fold the caboose bottom along the fold line. Referring to the diagram, pin the caboose bottom in place with the folded edge at the top. Align the left edges of the caboose pieces and align the bottom edge with the bottom edge of the coal car. Appliqué both the caboose top and bottom, stitching down the right edge, across the bottom, and up the left edges. (Leave the folded edges unstitched.)

8. Referring to the placement diagram, pin the large wheel in place. Appliqué, leaving the upper edge unstitched between marks, as indicated on the pattern. Pin small wheels ⅛″ below the bottom edge of the train. Appliqué all the way around each small wheel.

9. With raw edges aligned, stack the fleece and pindot rectangles (right side up). To form the large pocket, fold the ticking in half with wrong sides facing. Baste the raw edges together. Place the pocket (appliqué side up) on top of the pindot, aligning the side and bottom edges. Baste all the way around the caddy through all layers. Bind the edges with the bias tape, mitering the corners.

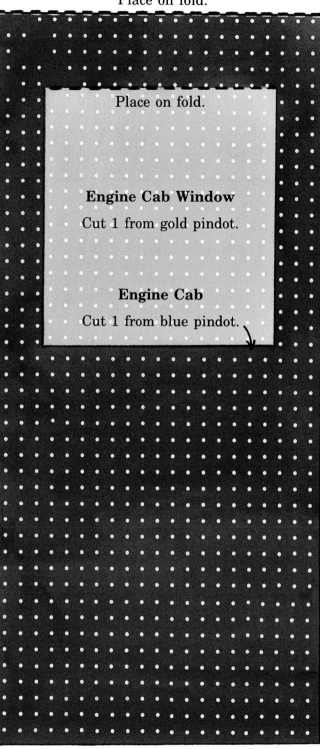

Place on fold.

Place on fold.

Engine Cab Window

Cut 1 from gold pindot.

Engine Cab

Cut 1 from blue pindot.

To divide the ticking pocket into 2 smaller pockets, topstitch where indicated on the diagram. (It will be necessary to fold the diagonal edge of the coal car back so that you don't stitch through it.)

Place on fold.

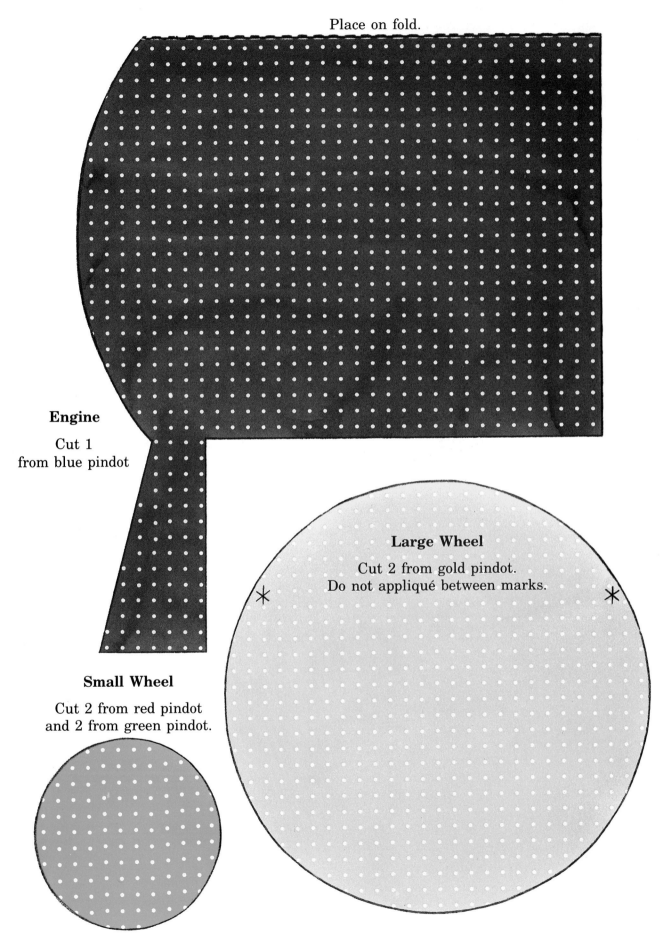

Engine

Cut 1
from blue pindot

Large Wheel

Cut 2 from gold pindot.
Do not appliqué between marks.

Small Wheel

Cut 2 from red pindot
and 2 from green pindot.

Caboose Top Cut 1 from red pindot.

Place on fold.

Place on fold.

Caboose Window

Cut 1 from gold pindot.

Place on fold.

Coal Car

Cut 1 from green pindot.

Place on fold.

Caboose Bottom

Cut 1 from red pindot.

123

Stocking Cap Cuties

A soft, huggable toy is always a favorite with little ones. This one is quick and easy to make and just as easy to keep clean, since it's made from a machine-washable stocking cap. You might consider using baby's first stocking cap to make this cutie.

You will need:
Knitted (acrylic yarn) stocking cap with a
    double thickness and ear flaps
Thread to match
Lining fabric (optional)
Polyester stuffing
Darning needle and quilting thread
Black embroidery floss

1. Carefully snip threads to remove ear flaps, ties, and pom-pom (if there is one) from the stocking cap.

2. Turn the cap wrong side out. Near the top of the cap, insert the scissors and carefully cut all the way around the lining, being careful not to cut into the outer layer of the cap. (Figure A.) Gently pull the lining down out of the cap to form a cylinder. (Cap will now be almost twice its original length.) (Figure B.)

3. Turn the cylinder so that the opening is at the top. To form the head, draw a curved line about ⅓ of the way down. Stitch. (Figure C.) Repeat for the other side. Leave the top of the head unstitched. Trim the seams to ⅛″ and turn cap right side out.

4. If the cap is made of a loosely woven or very thin knit, you'll need to line it. Fold the lining fabric in half. Place the cap on top of the lining and trace around it, adding a ¼″ seam allowance. Cut out. With right sides facing, stitch the lining pieces together, leaving the top of the head unstitched. Turn right side out and slip the lining inside the cap.

5. Stuff (if lined, place stuffing in lining) until firm and flat. Whipstitch the opening closed.

6. To define the neck, run a line of stitches by hand around the neck and pull to gather. Sew together the unknotted ends of the 2 cap ties. Tie in a bow around the neck.

7. To shape the legs and arms, use the needle and quilting thread to hand-stitch through all layers. (Figure D.)

8. For ears, hand-stitch the cap ear flaps to the top of the head.

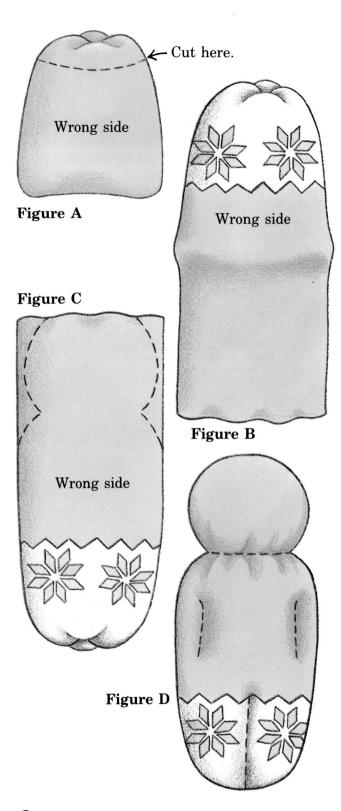

Figure A

Figure B

Figure C

Figure D

9. Using 6 strands of black floss, satin-stitch the eyes and nose. Backstitch the whiskers and mouth. If the cap had a pom-pom, stitch it securely on for a tail.

Bear Necessities

Bear in mind—you might find the kids talking to the furniture when chairs are dressed in these pink and blue cover-ups.

You will need (for each chair):
¾ yard polka-dot fabric
8″ square of white fabric
Fabric scraps for eyes and nose
Thread to match fabrics
Paper-backed fusible web
½ yard thick batting
½ yard thermal lining
3 yards of white piping
3⅓ yards (⅜″-wide) white ribbon
⅝ yard (1″-wide) ribbon

Note: All seam allowances are ½″.

Figure A

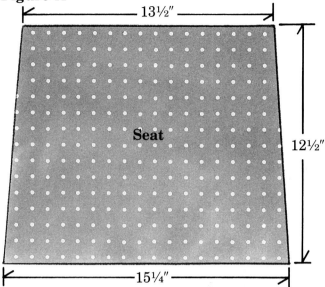

1. Trace and cut out patterns. For the chair back, cut 2 (13½″) squares from the polka-dot fabric, 1 from batting, and 1 from thermal lining. For the seat, cut 2 pieces from polka-dot as shown in the diagram. (Figure A.) Cut 1 seat from batting and 1 from thermal lining. Cut the ears as marked.

2. According to the manufacturers' directions, fuse the web to the wrong side of the white fabric and fabric scraps. Trace the ear, ear center, eyes, nose, and muzzle patterns onto the paper side of the web. Cut out.

3. Remove the paper backing from the appliqué shapes. Fuse the ear centers in place as shown on the pattern. Place the bottom edge of the muzzle 2½″ from the bottom edge and 3½″ from the side edges of the chair back. (Figure B.) Fuse in place. Using white thread, machine-appliqué the muzzle and 2 ear centers. With matching thread, appliqué the eyes and nose. Using thread to match the bear, satin-stitch the mouth and outline-stitch around the muzzle and ear centers. Press.

Figure B

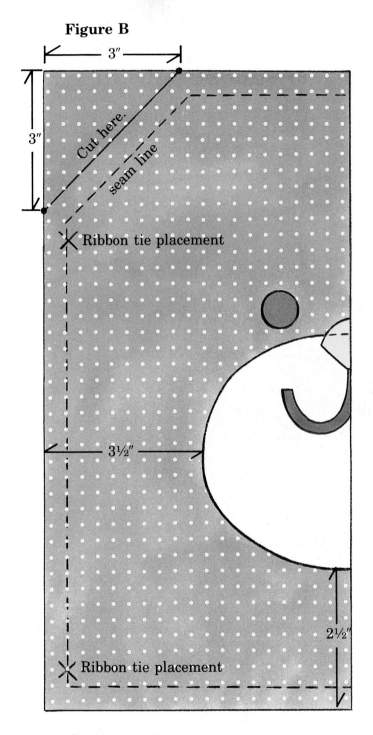

3″

3″

Cut here.

seam line

✕ Ribbon tie placement

3½″

2½″

✕ Ribbon tie placement

4. To shape the top corners of the bear's head, start at a top corner on the appliquéd piece and measure 3″ down the side. Mark. From the same corner, measure 3″ along the top of the head and mark. Draw

a diagonal line connecting the marks. Cut along this line. (Figure B.) Use the cutaway piece as a pattern and trim the other front corner and 2 corners of the back, batting, and lining.

5. To make 1 ear, stack in this order: batting, ear front, and ear back (right sides facing). Stitch around the ear through all layers, leaving the bottom edge open. Clip and turn right side out. Baste the opening closed. With the appliquéd side of the ear down and raw edges aligned, baste the ear to the right side of the bear's head at the trimmed corner. Repeat for the other ear.

6. For ties, cut 12 (10″) pieces of white ribbon. Baste the ends of 4 pairs of ribbons to the front of the bear's head as indicated on the diagram. (Figure B.) Baste a pair of ribbons at each back corner of the chair seat.

7. To attach piping, use a zipper foot to sew close to the edge of the cording. With right sides together and raw edges aligned, machine-stitch the piping along the edges of the back pieces of the chair back and chair seat.

8. To assemble the chair back, pin the ribbons and ears toward the center. Stack the pieces in this order: batting, thermal lining, front (right side up), back (right side down). With raw edges aligned, stitch on the stitching line of the piping. Leave an opening in 1 side for turning. Clip the corners, turn, and press. Slipstitch the opening closed. Repeat for the chair seat. Tie a bow with the 1″-wide ribbon and whipstitch in place on the bear face (see photo).

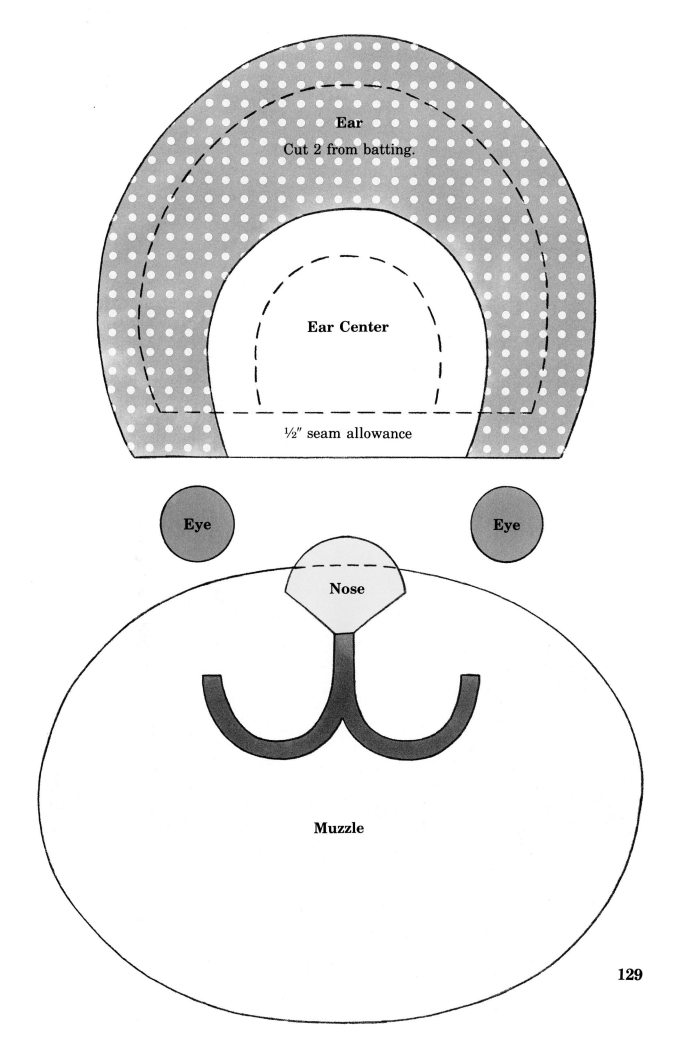

Ear

Cut 2 from batting.

Ear Center

½″ seam allowance

Eye

Eye

Nose

Muzzle

129

Clown Bookends

Send in the clowns to support the reading habit. Books once scattered from here to there will become upright and organized between these colorful clowns.

You will need:
Tracing paper
Graphite paper
Pencil
2 (8″) pieces of 1 x 4 pine (for uprights)
1 (15″) piece of 1 x 6 pine (for clowns)
Scroll or jigsaw

Sandpaper: medium and fine grit
Acrylic paints: pink, red, blue, orange, green, white, yellow, black
Paintbrushes: ⅜″ flat, and small fine pointed
Acrylic spray
Drill with ¹⁄₁₆″ countersink drill bits
2 (3⅛″ x 5″) nail plates
8 (⅛″ x 1½″) flat wood screws
Screwdriver

1. Trace the clown pattern and cut out. Transfer it twice to the 1 x 6. Cut out both clowns using the scroll saw.

2. Sand all sides of the clowns and the 1 x 4 uprights with both grades of sandpaper, beginning with medium.

3. With the flat paintbrush, paint a pink base coat on all 4 pieces. Let dry; then sand lightly. Paint all sides of the uprights red. Using graphite paper, transfer the clown's features to 1 clown. Reverse the pattern and turn over the other clown; then transfer the features. Referring to the pattern, paint the clowns as indicated, letting the paint dry between coats. Use the fine-pointed brush to paint the small details.

4. Spray each piece with several coats of acrylic, letting it dry between coats.

5. To assemble, center the 3⅛″ end of 1 nail plate under and perpendicular to the end of 1 upright (see Figure). Drill 2 starter holes into the bottom of the upright through the holes on either side of the center hole of the nail plate. Screw the plate to the upright. Repeat for the other upright.

6. To attach 1 clown, mark the center of the palm of each hand. Then make 2 corresponding marks down the center of 1 upright. Drill a hole through each mark on the upright. Hold the clown against the upright on the side opposite the nail plate. Be sure that the clown's feet are level with the bottom edge of the upright/nail plate unit. From the inside of the upright, screw through the lower hole into the clown's lower hand. Then screw through the upper hole into the clown's upper hand. Repeat for the other bookend.

Figure—Alignment of Upright and Nail Plate

Clown

Dreamland Dragon

This dragon sleeping bag takes a bit of time, but it's all basic sewing. And when outstretched arms welcome your sleepyhead to a dreamland filled with adventures, you'll know your time was well spent.

You will need:
Tracing paper
8 yards (45″-wide) green fabric
3½ yards of quilt batting
¼ yard (45″-wide) yellow fabric
¼ yard red fabric
Paper-backed fusible web
1¾ yards (45″-wide) blue-striped fabric
Thread to match fabrics
Water-soluble marker
2 (1¼″) yellow buttons
2 yards of Velcro
Polyester stuffing
½ yard (¼″-wide) red ribbon

Note: Use ¼″ seam allowances throughout except when instructed otherwise.

Making the Head

1. Trace the nose section of the head pattern, aligning the right edge of the tracing paper with the fold line of the pattern. To complete the head pattern, refer to Figure A for shape and measurements. Transfer patterns and markings for tongue, nostril, and cheek, and cut as marked.

2. Cut 2 heads from the green fabric and 1 head from the batting. Cut 2 tongues from the yellow fabric and 1 from batting. Cut 2 heart cheeks from red fabric and 2 from fusible web. Cut 2 nostrils from the striped fabric and 2 from the fusible web. For ears, cut 2 (12″) squares from the green fabric and 1 (5″) square from the yellow fabric. For points between ears, cut 6 (7″) squares from the striped fabric.

3. To make the tongue, stack the front and back pieces with right sides together. Place the batting piece on the bottom. Stitch around the 2 sides, leaving the base of the triangle open as indicated on the pattern. Clip tips and trim excess batting from the seam. Turn right side out. Press. With right sides facing and raw edges aligned, center the tongue on the front of the nose with the tip of the tongue toward the face. Baste in place.

4. Following the manufacturer's directions, fuse the web to the wrong side of the nostrils. Remove the paper backing and fuse the nostrils in place on the nose (see pattern). Fuse the web to the wrong side of the cheeks. Remove the paper backing and fuse the cheeks in place on the head, 4¾″ up from the nose line and ¾″ from the center fold. (Figure A.) Using white thread, machine-appliqué the nostrils and cheeks in place. With the marker, draw curved lines connecting the tips of the heart cheeks with the sides of the face.

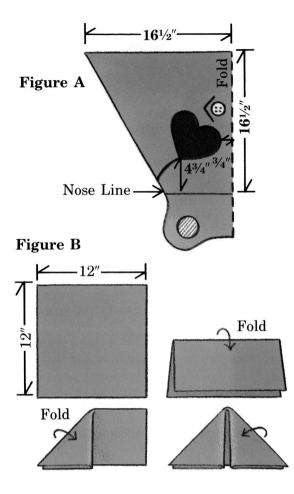

Figure A

Figure B

5. Stack the batting, head front (right side up), and head back (right side down). Using ½″ seam, stitch together, catching the tongue in the seam and leaving the straight edge at the top of the head open. Clip curves, trim excess batting from the seams, and turn right side out. Press.

6. With the water-soluble marker, draw a vertical quilting line along the fold line of the head. Measure 2″ on each side of this line and draw another line. Continue marking lines across the head every 2″. (Do not draw through the cheeks or the nostrils.) Beginning at the nose and ending about 1″ from the top of the head, machine-quilt through all the layers along the marked lines. (Do not quilt over cheeks or nostrils.) Using red thread, zig-zag-stitch the lines from the cheeks to the sides of the head. Using black thread, zig-zag-stitch the eyebrows. Sew on the yellow button eyes. (Figure A.)

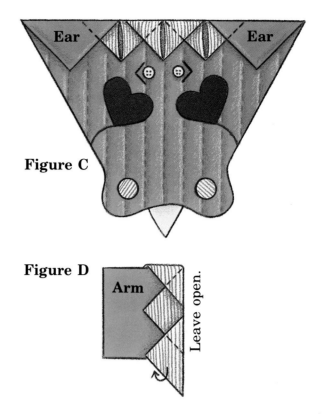

Figure C

7. To make ears, fold a 12″ green square in half with wrong sides facing. Then fold the 2 corners on the folded edge to the bottom center to form a triangle. (Figure B.) Press. Cut the yellow square in half diagonally to form 2 triangles. Matching the bases and aligning the points, center 1 yellow triangle on the folded side of the green triangle. Baste the bases together. With white thread, appliqué around the remaining 2 sides of the yellow triangle. Repeat to make the second ear, using the remaining green square and remaining yellow triangle.

8. To make the points between the dragon's ears, fold the striped squares the same way you folded the squares for the ears. Press. With raw edges aligned and folded sides up, pin 3 points along the top of the head. Align the tip of the center point with the vertical center of the head. (Figure C.) Baste in place. With raw edges aligned, pin the ears right side down, overlapping the 2 outer points as shown. Baste the ears in place. With folded sides down, pin 2 of the remaining points on top of the left and right basted points, sandwiching the corners of the ears between. Lay the last point in the center, and baste the points in place.

Making the Fingers, Hands, Arms

1. For the fingers, cut 6 (8″) squares from the striped fabric. Fold as you did the ears. Press.

2. For the hands, cut 2 (4½″ x 16½″) green rectangles. To make a tube, stitch the ends together with right sides facing and raw edges aligned. Center the seam on 1 side of the hand and press the seam allowance in 1 direction. Do not turn. Repeat with the remaining rectangle.

Figure D

3. For the arms, cut 2 (6½″ x 16½″) green rectangles. To make tubes, repeat Step 2 for hands. Turn right side out.

4. To attach fingers, center 1 finger, folded side down, on the right side of 1 arm, aligning raw edges. Align the folds of the other 2 fingers with the edges of the tube, overlapping the first finger and wrapping to the other side of the tube. (Figure D.) Baste the fingers in place. (Do not stitch the end of the tube closed.) Attach the remaining 3 fingers to the other arm in the same manner.

5. To join the hand to the arm, slip 1 hand tube over 1 arm tube, with right sides facing. With seams matching, align the raw edges of the fingers and arm with 1 raw edge of the hand. Stitch around the tube along the basted edge. Turn the entire tube wrong side out. Stitch across the open end of the hand. Clip the corners and turn right side out. Fold the fingers toward the hand. Press flat. Join the other hand and arm in the same manner.

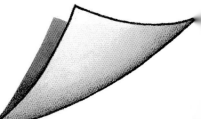

6. To mark an arm for quilting, draw a line from the base of the middle finger up the center of the arm to the raw edge. (Do not mark the fingers or the hand.) Draw additional lines every 2″ on each side of the center line. Mark the other arm in the same way.

Cut 2 (8″ x 9½″) pieces of batting to fit inside the arm/hand units. Slip 1 piece of batting inside 1 arm/hand unit. Beginning at the base of the middle finger and stitching to the raw edge of the arm, machine-quilt along the marked lines through all layers. Repeat for the other arm.

Making the Tail

1. Transfer the pattern for the tail tip and cut out. Cut 2 (13″-diameter) circles from the striped fabric. Fold each circle in half and then in half again. Place the pattern on 1 circle, making sure the fold lines of the pattern are on the folds of the fabric. Cut out 1 tip from each circle. Cut an 8½″ x 46½″ strip from the green fabric for the tail. Cut 6 (8″) squares from the striped fabric for the points.

2. Fold the squares as before to make 6 points. With right sides facing and raw edges aligned, pin the points along 1 long edge of the tail, overlapping the points ½″. Baste. With right sides facing, stitch the tail together along the long edges and across 1 end. Clip corners and turn right side out. Stuff firmly. Baste the open end closed.

3. With right sides facing and raw edges aligned, stitch the 2 striped tail tips together, leaving a 2″ opening on the side of 1 point. Clip corners and turn right side out. Stuff lightly. Slipstitch the opening closed. To attach the tip to the tail, topstitch the stitched end of the tail to the middle of the tail tip.

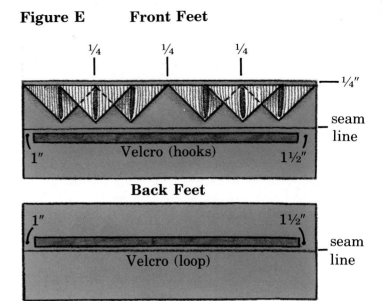

Figure E   **Front Feet**

¼   ¼   ¼

¼″

seam line

1″   Velcro (hooks)   1½″

Back Feet

1″   1½″

Velcro (loop)

seam line

Making the Feet and Toes

1. Cut 4 (32″ x 4½″) strips from the green fabric for the feet. Cut 6 (8″) squares from the striped fabric for the toes. Fold the squares as before to make 6 toes.

2. With right sides facing, stitch 2 strips together along 1 (32″) edge. Press the seam in 1 direction. Repeat with the other 2 strips.

3. Open 1 strip and place it right side up. Divide 1 long edge of the strip into quarters and mark. Pin 6 toes in place as shown, with folded sides up, and raw edges ¼″ from the raw edge of the strip. (Figure E.) Baste.

4. For the front feet, begin 1″ from the left side of the strip/toe unit and sew 29½″ of Velcro (hook side) to the right side of the strip, just below the seam line. (Figure E.) For back feet, open the second strip and place it right side up. Beginning 1″ from the left edge, stitch 29½″ of Velcro (loop side) just above the seam line. (Figure E.)

5. Cut 2 (31″ x 4″) strips from batting for the feet. Set aside.

Making the Body Back

1. Cut 2 (32″ x 54½″) green rectangles. Cut 1 (31″ x 53″) rectangle from batting. Cut 6 (8″) squares from striped fabric.

2. To mark the right side of 1 green rectangle for quilting, draw a line down the lengthwise center. Continue marking lines every 2″.

3. Stack the unmarked rectangle (right side down), batting (centered on the rectangle), and the marked rectangle (right side up). Pin together. Machine-quilt along the marked lines, starting each line of stitching 1½″ from the top. Leave 2″ unquilted on outside edges.

4. To attach the back feet, place right sides together and align a 32″ edge of the body back with the 32″ edge of the back feet farthest from the loop Velcro. Using ½″ seam, stitch along this edge. Press seam allowance toward feet. Press under ½″ of the unstitched 32″ edge.
Fold the back feet with wrong sides together, and slip the batting piece between. Leaving ½″ unstitched on each side, slipstitch the pressed edge to the inside of the body back along the seam line.

5. Place the body back with Velcro side down. Fold the striped squares as before to make 6 points. With raw edges aligned and folded side up, place the first point along the right edge ½″ from the top. Add the remaining points, overlapping the points ½″. Baste in place. (Figure F.)

6. Baste the end of the tail to left side of the body back, directly above the seam for the feet. (Figure F.)

7. To attach the head, separate the top 1½″ of the pieces of the body back, pinning the inside piece aside. Then pin the

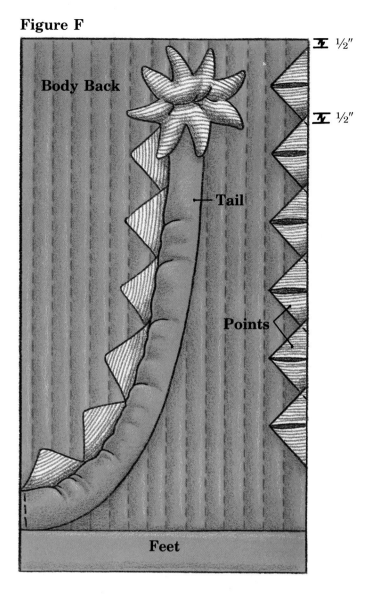

Figure F

head, face side down and straight edges aligned, to the outside body back. Stitch, using ½″ seam. Press the seam allowance toward the body and the head away from the body.
Replace the inside body back. Turn under the seam allowance on the top edge and topstitch along the fold through all layers. Finish quilting the 1½″ left unstitched at the top edge (see Step 3).

8. Cut a 1½″ x 57″ strip from the green fabric. Turn under ¼″ on 1 end. Press. With right sides facing, raw edges aligned, and the turned-under end even with the bottom of the left side of the outside body back, stitch the strip and back together, using ½″ seam. Turn under the top edge of the strip to match the top of the body. Turn under ¼″ on the remaining long edge of the strip. Press. Fold the strip to inside of the body back to encase the seam allowance and baste in place.

Pin 38″ of the loop Velcro to the strip, beginning at the bottom of the feet, aligning the right edges. Topstitch the Velcro and strip in place.

Making the Body Front

1. Cut 2 (32″ x 36½″) green rectangles. Cut 1 (31″ x 35″) rectangle from batting.

2. To quilt the body front, repeat Steps 2 and 3 of Making the Body Back but begin quilting at the top edge.

3. To give the appearance of legs, pin 1 end of the ribbon to the outside body front at the center of the bottom edge. Pin the ribbon up the front, turning under ¼″ at the top. Topstitch in place.

4. Stitch the feet/toe unit to the bottom outside body front, following directions in Step 4 of Making the Body Back.

5. To finish the top edge, fold under ¼″ and then fold under another ⅜″. Machine-stitch close to the first folded edge.

6. With right sides facing and raw edges and top edges aligned, lay 1 arm on the left edge of the outside body front. Baste in place. Repeat for the other arm.

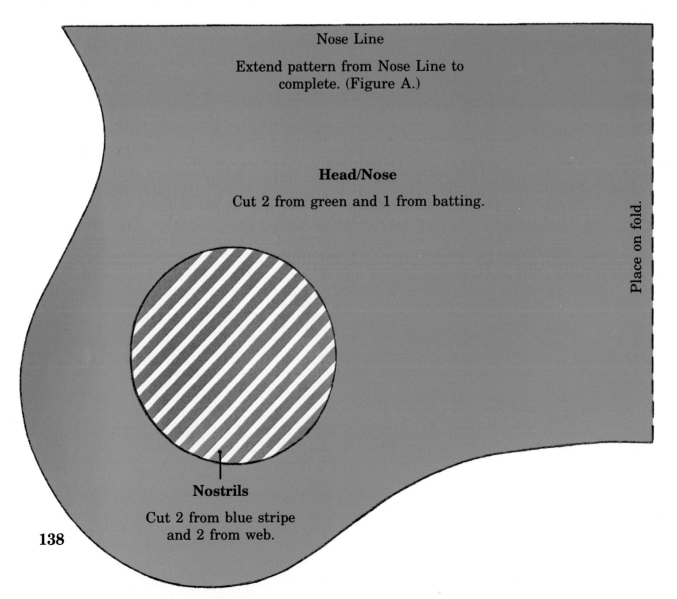

Nose Line

Extend pattern from Nose Line to complete. (Figure A.)

Head/Nose

Cut 2 from green and 1 from batting.

Place on fold.

Nostrils

Cut 2 from blue stripe and 2 from web.

7. Cut a 1½″ x 39″ green strip. Follow Step 8 of Making the Body Back to stitch the strip to the right side of the outside body front, and to stitch the hook Velcro to the strip.

8. Pin the raw edge of the inside body back out of the way. Then, with right sides facing and feet and raw edges aligned, pin together the raw edges of the body front and outside body back, with the arm and points to the center. Stitch, using ½″ seam. Be sure not to catch the inside body back in the seam. Press the seam toward the body back. Press under the seam allowance on the inside body back and topstitch close to folded edge through all layers.

Cheeks
Cut 2 from red and 2 from web.

Place on fold.

Tip of Tail

Cut 2 from blue stripe.

Place on fold.

Tongue

Cut 2 from yellow and 1 from batting.

Place on fold.

A Lovable Lamb

With a little wood, a few tools, and some bright-colored paints, you can create a playful little lamb that, just like Mary's, will follow its owner wherever he goes.

You will need:
Tracing paper
Yardstick
¾″ plywood (18″ x 4 feet)
Scrap of black suede leather
Electric saber saw
1 (15″-long) pine 2 x 6 for platform
1 (12″-long) pine 1 x 4
¼″ electric drill
Electric drill bits: ¹⁄₁₆″, ⅛″, ¼″, ⅜″
⅜″ brad-point wood bit
Hole saw for electric drill
Wood filler
Sandpaper (medium and fine grade)
White enamel primer spray
Acrylic paints: white, black, red, green,
    blue-gray
Paintbrushes
Wood clamps
#6 drywall screws: 8 (1¼″), 4 (1″)
4 (2½″) #12 round-head screws with
    threadless upper shaft
Countersink bit
8 washers with ¼″ holes
1 large screw eye
20″ nylon cord for pull
14″ (1″-wide) ribbon
Cow bell

Making the Lamb

1. Trace and cut out patterns for the lamb body, leg, and ear.

2. Trace the ear pattern on the leather and cut out. On the plywood, trace around the pattern for the lamb's body and 4 legs. Make sure the bottom of each leg is positioned along the factory edge of the plywood.

3. Using the saber saw, cut out the body and legs of the lamb. Using the electric drill and hole saw, cut 4 wheels with 2″ diameters and ¼″ center holes from the pine 1 x 4. Also from the 1 x 4, cut 2 spacer blocks, each ¾″ wide and 2″ long.

4. For the ear hole, drill through the head with the ¹⁄₁₆″ bit where indicated on the pattern. Then, lining up the point of the ⅜″ brad-point wood bit with the ¹⁄₁₆″ hole, drill only halfway through the hole. Turn the lamb over and drill through the other half of the hole. (Drilling from both sides keeps wood from splintering.)

5. Use wood filler to fill any imperfections in the wood or gaps in the edges of the plywood. Let dry. Sand filler and all edges smooth.

6. Spray all pieces (both sides and all edges) with white enamel primer. Let dry and sand lightly. Paint the lamb white. Paint the top of the platform and spacer blocks green. Paint the side of the platform red as shown. Paint the wheels and legs black. (See photo.) Apply several coats of paint to all pieces, letting the paint dry between coats.

7. When the final coat of paint is dry, transfer facial features and curls to the body. Paint as shown in photo. If desired, lighten the blue-gray paint with white for the curls. Mix red and white paint for the cheeks. They may require 2 coats. Use 1 coat for the other details.

Assembling the Lamb

1. For the front legs, place 1 leg on top of a second and align the edges; clamp together. Drill ⅛″ hole through both legs as indicated on the pattern. Repeat for back legs. Drill ⅛″ holes through the body as indicated on the pattern. Attach the legs to the body with the 1″ drywall screws. Countersink the screw heads. Fill the countersink holes with wood filler. Let dry and sand lightly.

2. Draw a line lengthwise down the center of the platform. Center spacer blocks lengthwise on this line, 1 block 2½″ from the back, and 1 block 3½″ from the front. To secure the blocks to the platform, use 2 (1¼″) drywall screws in each block. Countersink the screw heads.

3. Fit the lamb's feet down over the spacer blocks. Secure them to the blocks by countersinking and passing a 1¼″ drywall screw from the outside of each foot into the block. Fill the countersink holes with wood filler. Let dry and sand lightly.

4. To attach the wheels, on 1 side of the platform mark a drill hole ½″ from the bottom edge and 2″ from the front edge. Mark another 2″ from the back edge. Mark the opposite side of the platform with the same measurements. Drill ⅛″ holes through each mark. Pass a #12 round-head screw through a washer, a wheel, another washer, and into the ⅛″ hole in the platform. Tighten the screw until the wheel will rotate freely but not wobble. Attach the remaining 3 wheels in the same manner.

5. Repaint any areas that need touching up. Let dry.

6. To attach the ear, tightly roll up the ear lengthwise. Gently push half of it through the hole in the lamb's head, so that the ears hang freely on both sides.

7. Mark the center front of the platform. Insert the screw eye. For a pull, attach the nylon cord to the screw eye. Knot the other end of the cord. Slip the ribbon through the cowbell and tie it around the lamb's neck.

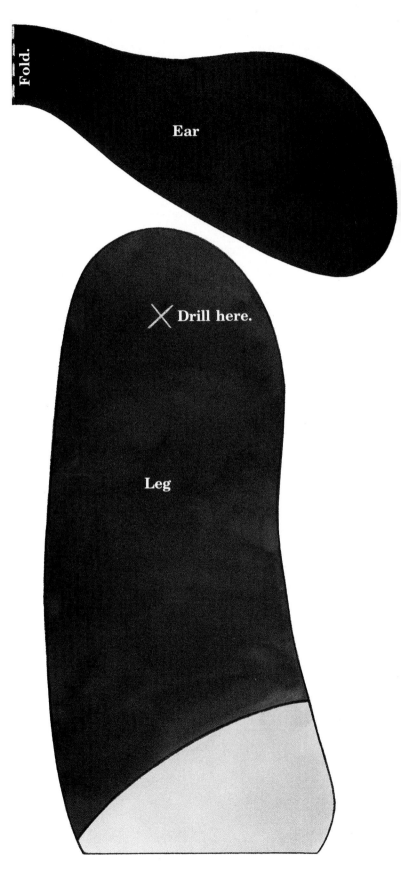

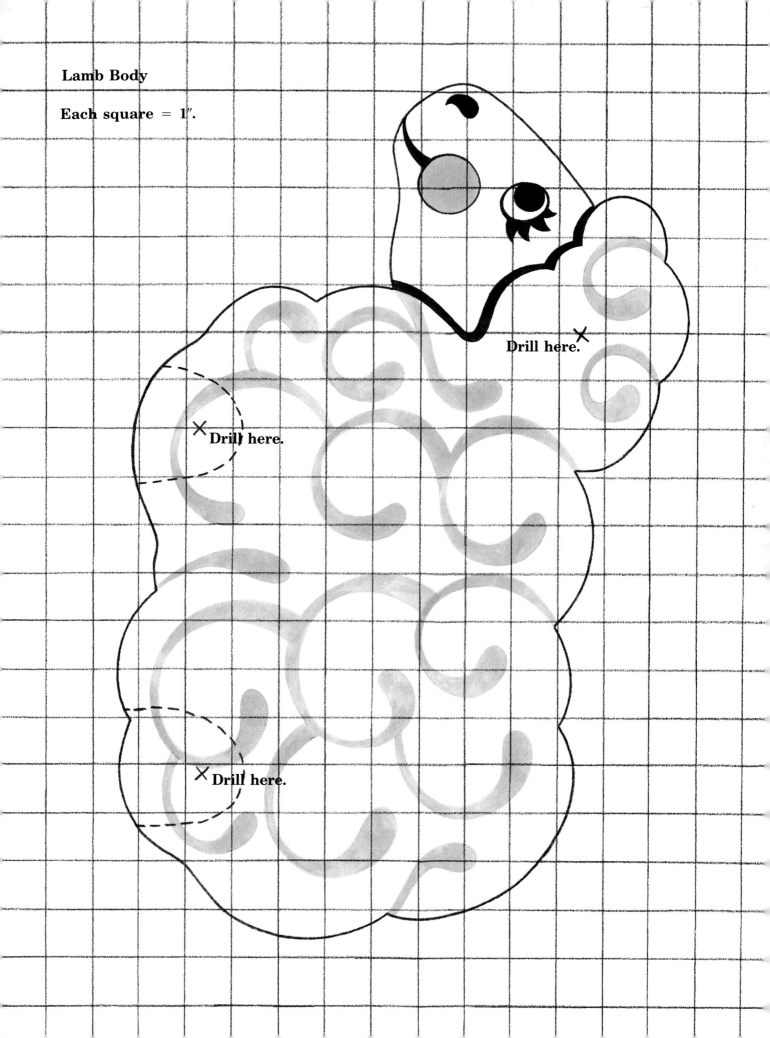

Lamb Body

Each square = 1″.

Drill here.

Drill here.

Drill here.

Designers & Contributors

Marina Anderson, Winter Sweats, 95; P. J. Pooch, 99; Wagon Dragon, 101; Cow Clock, 114; Bear Necessities, 126.

Barbara Ball, A Lovable Lamb (painting and design), 140.

Amy Albert Bloom, Santa Card Box, 56.

Patricia Channell, Stocking Cap Cuties, 124.

Sharon Christman, Deer, Deer!, 26.

Alice L. Cox, costume designs for *The Littlest Star*, 18; Holly Days Skirt & Sweater, 89.

Hope Crawford, Bedtime Caddy, 119.

Connie Formby, ticket and program for *The Littlest Star*, 20, 21; Stars 'n Straws, 33; Walk on the Wild Side, 84.

Lindsey Franklin, Safety Pin Bracelets, 70.

Joyce M. Gillis, Woven Santa Basket, 45; Winter Flurry Windsock, 53; Family Tree, 75.

Linda Hendrickson, Three Kings Card, 48; Christmas Tree Watering Can, 60; Pig E. Bank, 62; Paw Pad, 72; Clown Bookends, 130; Dreamland Dragon, 132.

Connie Matricardi, Christmas Brigade, 28.

Walter M. Rush, Jr., A Lovable Lamb (construction), 140.

Linda Martin Stewart, Funky Frames, 78.

Mollie Jane Taylor, Smocked Christmas Packages, 82.

Carol M. Tipton, Button-Face Angels, 30; Straw Garlands, 34; Feathered Friends, 37; Nativity Puzzle, 104; Travel Tic-Tac-Toe, 110.

Janice Weinstein, Stars & Bars Sweater, 92.

Eileen Westfall, Baseball Card Bag, 68.

Madeline O'Brien White, A Hands-Some Wreath, 40; Snowbuddies, 42; Tear It Up, 50; Balloon Bow, 66.

Patricia Dreame Wilson, author of *The Littlest Star*, 8.

Special thanks to the following shops in Birmingham, Alabama, for sharing their resources: **Applause Dancewear & Accessories; Chocolate Soup, Inc.; Ed's Pet World; Huffstutler's Hardware Home Center; Jack N' Jill Shop; Kiddieland Shop; New Environs, Inc.; Playfair, Inc.; Ray's Children's Shop; Virginia Kelso; Sikes Children's Shoes; Smith's Variety of Mountain Brook; Vestavia Hills Apothecary.**